the ADVANCEMENT

the ADVANCEMENT

KEEPING THE FAITH IN AN EVOLUTIONARY AGE

L. RUSS BUSH

BROADMAN
&HOLMAN
PUBLISHERS

NASHVILLE, TENNESSEE

0–8054–3034–2

Published by Broadman & Holman Publishers,
Nashville, Tennessee

Dewey Decimal Classification: 210
Subject Heading: NATURAL THEOLOGY \
CHRISTIANITY—RELATIONS—NATURAL THEOLOGY

Unless otherwise noted, Scripture quotations are from the Holy
Bible, New International Version, copyright © 1973, 1978, 1984
by International Bible Society.

2 3 4 5 6 7 8 9 10 08 07 06 05 04 03

Dedication

to

Cindy

Josh and Beth

John 17:9

CONTENTS

PREFACE

OUR AGE is not what it used to be. We are now living in an age of advancement. The Christian consensus no longer dominates Western civilization. We have grown so used to the "new" as being the best solution to whatever "the problem" is that we can hardly appreciate the past anymore, and it is very difficult to recognize or evaluate what is significant.

We did not lose our intellectual blend of biblical ideas and Christian standards overnight, but it is clear that we have lost the Western cultural consensus that understood and appreciated biblical truth and values. How did that happen? What exactly has replaced it? Why do so many seem to misunderstand the Christian witness today? Who would have thought that persecution would be so strong against Christians in the modern world?

The fact is, many Americans and Europeans and others have simply adopted naturalistic philosophy in place of a theistic worldview, and the consequences are showing up everywhere. This is that about which I have tried to write! Illusion is the new "reality." Evolution is the new "fact" around which all knowledge is evaluated. Meaning no longer means what we though it meant. Courts no longer rule according to original intent. Even our Preachers no longer seem to know for sure what a biblical passage actually teaches. Decisions seem to be *ad hoc,* and moral standards seem to be relative. Where did this new approach to life come from, and why did things change so drastically from one generation (pre-1950) to the next (post-1975)?

The publisher decided to move all of my footnotes to the end, supposedly to make the pages "more readable." Some of my better arguments are found in those notes, and a good deal of supplementary information is found there. For my students, I tried to use the notes to remind them of important bibliographical sources where they could do further research on key points. Readers who ignore the notes will get the gist of things, but I urge the old "keep one finger in the back" technique for serious readers. Many important ideas are unfortunately hidden away in those endnotes.

Chapter 1 outlines the worldview that dominates our day, contrasting it with the parallel elements of the older Christian worldview. We find that "inevitable progress" has replaced the "stability" that Christian culture found in an unchanging God. I have coined the term "the Advancement" as a name for this new worldview. Our contemporary generation believes that it is living in an age of progress in every aspect of life. The "Enlightenment" thinkers of the eighteenth century were quite confident that their understanding of the world was vastly superior to that of scholars in the so-called "dark" ages. In a similar way, many today accept the notion that the modern world is on the move, not only with advancements in technology, but that in spite of terrorism and other threats, we are progressing toward world peace and intellectual freedom and political tolerance. We think we are advancing in every way. It will be our task to examine this notion.

Chapter 2 focuses on the rise of modern science. By no means would I suggest that all scientists are philosophical naturalists, but naturalism is the dominant methodology of the Advancement. Chapter 3 illustrates the fundamental flaw in philosophical naturalism. Truth and even knowledge itself are both threatened by naturalistic thinking. What an unexpected result! And yet, what a critical insight! Biological evolution, the so-called "most assured fact" of "Advancement" philosophy is also the "fact" that most threatens the viability of all knowledge. This surely must cause us to pause in the midst of such sweeping change for a little "re-evaluation."

Chapter 4 considers several current "redefinitions" of God that supposedly avoid the dire consequences revealed in Chapter Three. Modern science has a new view of physics, so why should modern philosophy not have a new metaphysics? Maybe God himself is a dynamic process like the creation seems to be. Would this not solve many intellectual problems? The answer, however, is no. This new God is not the real God. "Open theism" supposedly takes advantage of modern ideas about physics and metaphysics, but this new proposal remains speculative, for by definition it cannot be grounded on a firm foundation. The God of "open theism" may find Himself to be wrong about the actual future; therefore, those who trusted Him would be found to be lacking the truth.

At the heart of the modern world is the theory of naturalistic evolution. Chapter 5 seeks to expose the theory behind the theory, and chapter 6 explains why the theory fails in its naturalistic form. In chapter 7, the bigger point is made that Advancement philosophy as a whole is not only a failure intellectually but that it is ultimately an illusion. Inevitable progress is not the order of the day. An unchanging God still rules.

Chapter 8 asks the final question: "What Then Are We to Believe?" My answer is traditional. God exists necessarily, the world exists contingently, and Jesus Christ is Lord, whether we think so or not. God sets the rules of the game. Our freedom (and thus our significance) is exclusively based on His freedom. No freedom (and no significance) comes from naturalism.

* * * * * * *

One of the joys of my life has been the opportunity to work for almost thirty years in an academic environment. Seminary students come in all flavors, but each one makes their mark somewhere in the world; and a student's mark is an expression of the impression a Faculty makes on him or her. Being only one member of a large

Faculty sufficiently dilutes one's self-promoting ego, and yet the classroom remains a most satisfying place to work.

This volume has been shared in pieces with my students over a good many years. Only recently has it come together in publishable form. I am grateful for the many valuable insights I have gained from those who interacted with earlier drafts of some of these pages. I don't blame them for my remaining errors or for my resistance to correction.

I have no accurate list of everyone who over several years helped to type, edit, and format portions of this manuscript, but I must mention Amanda Hodge and Melanie Dunn, both of whom gave a good bit of time to the latter stages of this project. I do not mean to slight anyone by mentioning only these most recent secretarial assistants.

My wife, Cindy, is well aware of the many early a.m. hours it takes to find the time to compose, edit, and finish a project like this. She is the best person God ever sent into my life, and a great deal of what should have been "her time" is hidden away in the pages of this book. Perhaps a reader will one day think to thank her in addition to my expressed gratefulness here.

Overjoyed and humbled am I to present this little essay to a readership that inevitably will face the issues I address here. If one or seven find insight and help in these pages, it will have been worth the effort. Beyond that, the Lord only knows. It is comforting to rest such things in His hands.

L. Russ Bush
Southeastern Seminary
May 29, 2003

INTRODUCTION

GOD RULES OVER HUMAN HISTORY, and he alone determines its final result. His ways are not our ways, and his thoughts are not our thoughts, but we are made in his image. Thus, we are rational and spiritual beings, capable of moral discernment, able to communicate and able to understand those of his ways and thoughts that God chooses to reveal to us.

God has revealed himself by the act of creating. Had he not created something, his presence and character would not have been revealed or made known by anything or to anything other than himself in his Trinitarian nature. The world he created is orderly, beautiful, useful, full of energetic power, yet stable and meaningful (cf. Rom. 1:20). Had he not created sensual beings, God would have remained hidden and invisible, for his manifestations would have been unperceived and not understood by anyone other than himself. Seemingly there is little point in manifesting yourself only to yourself; so God, for reasons fully known only to himself, created beings like himself, beings who could know and be known, beings who could love and be loved, beings who could think, plan, and act. This creation of a "divine image" was history's beginning.[1]

Originally the setting for human life was by definition ideal. The newly created beings were in harmony with nature and with God, but the temptation of moral choice proved to be strong enough to disrupt that harmony. History took a sudden turn as innocence mutated into conflict and struggle.

1

The era of conscience[2] proved only that conscience was an insufficient barrier against wickedness. Conscience is an aspect of the divine image,[3] and through it God has revealed his moral standards (cf. Rom. 2), but conscience alone has insufficient power to force either universal or even simple majority compliance, and the power of the divinely created human will, fed by curiosity, led to an end, a conclusion, a final report. God did not destroy all of his precious creation, but his watery wrath fell upon a sinful world. Nevertheless, God's grace preserved human and young animal life in an ark, a floating hotel and zoo, a life-support system built to survive the great judgment by water.[4]

Civil law and governmental authority arose among this "family of the new beginning," but again the drive of human freedom led people to forget God. They began to worship created things rather than the Creator (cf. Rom. 1), and they sought to exalt themselves (Gen. 11).

God for a third time[5] began anew. He selected another family and a new means of making himself known to them. From Abraham onward, the requirement of faith and the willingness to see the truth and obey it became the focused element in biblical history. Two millennia before Christ, people worldwide were migrating and expanding their resources. In the midst of this dynamic era, God made specific promises to a new specific family that through them he would provide a way to restore the original harmony and bring lasting peace to an increasingly troubled world.

Eastern religious ideas became mystical and turned inward. The world itself was seen as a spiritual being, struggling to find harmony and integration. Traditional patterns held sway as the tested moral and social guides for life, and the civilizations of the East found themselves in never-ending time.[6] African tribal religions often rose beyond primitive animism, but the geography and ecology of the land so powerfully influenced the development of the region that cross-cultural achievements were rare. Western hemisphere tribal people also developed mystical religious ideas that guided their destiny, but in no case did these nature-oriented worldviews produce a lasting technology (other than, perhaps, some mathematical ideas and a few architectural feats that remain).[7]

The rise of Northern Mediterranean culture seems in the providence of God to have been the seedbed of the modern garden. The Greeks developed a group of schoolmen who began to demystify the world.[8] Their perspective was shaped by rational debate and careful observation. The Greek language was sophisticated and descriptively capable. The moral choices of individuals did not necessarily improve, but knowledge of the world did increase in many areas of political, philosophical, and scientific study.

Meanwhile, God had given his chosen descendants of Abraham a written revelation and a moral code. The Law, as it was called, guided the Israelite people of the Eastern Mediterranean through conflicts with Egypt, Assyria, Babylonia, and Persia. Alexander brought the Greek culture to Palestine as he passed through in 333 B.C., and then later Rome conquered and absorbed everything in the region for centuries.

During the days of Roman domination, God in an unexpected manner fulfilled his promise to that first sinful couple by personally coming to earth in the form of Christ and offering the ultimate payment to satisfy the divinely prescribed requirements for restoration and unity. Rome's power provided religious toleration[9] and security of travel, which in turn permitted new Christian believers to establish churches in many geographical locations. When Rome fell, the church through the next ten centuries maintained a significant portion of the knowledge that had been gained by that Roman civilization. This era of Charlemagne's Christendom is known today as the European Middle Ages.[10]

An attempt to restore classical Greco-Roman civilization motivated many in Europe to participate in a Renaissance and religiously in a Reformation. The new intellectual freedom, improved shipping and intercultural trade, growing technology, the discovery of the New World, the discovery of a new cosmology, better mapping techniques, and the printed page, along with rising literacy, propelled Europeans forward. The post-reformation movements, the age of reason, the Enlightenment era, and the so-called Romantic period all combined to produce the blend of ideas we recognize as the recent Modern era (nineteenth and twentieth centuries).[11]

A late twentieth-century shift,[12] an attempt to move beyond the "modern" era, has been dubbed by philosophers and literary scholars as the Postmodern era.[13] While this classification is not wrong as such, it has seemed to many that we cannot be in a postmodern world without playing word games, since most people think of "now" or "that which is current" as being the normal meaning of *modern.* The usage, however, is philosophical and refers to a new consciousness, an emphasis on fragmentation, strict relativism, and the loss of standard comprehensive worldviews that seems to be replacing the dominant naturalistic, scientific mind-set often associated with modernity. This change may be inevitable, but its value status is debatable. Meaningful discourse is struggling to survive. Relativism (irrationally) rules! Tolerance overwhelms significance. Naturalism still dominates in the scientific intellectual community, while Theism is disenfranchised.

Our civilization clearly is continuing to advance, however, in many important ways. Science and technology seem to be progressing faster than ever before. Our collective intelligent feeling is that we are on the verge of unprecedented breakthroughs in communications, space science, medical technology, materials science, and agriculture.

The twenty-first century era begs for a descriptive name. *Modern* seems strangely old-fashioned, and *Postmodern* is surely a temporary name. Perhaps the era through which we are passing could be dubbed the "Advancement." Modernism's tenants have not been thoroughly replaced in the popular culture, nor have even the intellectual elite fully abandoned them. Modernity still rules in many ways, but change is apparent. A sense of chaos seems to be creeping in, a sense of indeterminancy. Traditions are set aside; cultural roots are forgotten and ignored. In more ways than one, this is a new age, but the "new" is really "old." Nevertheless, the obvious technological progress must be recognized.

The challenge to divine authority is growing, and yet among Christians, a spirit of renewal is also growing. It is as if the wheat and the tares are nearing that anticipated final ripening stage, and a divine harvest is near. Intellectual leaders who guide the Christian community through these final days before the harvest must be able to discern the dangers of intellectual compromise. The church has greater spiritual power than all of her enemies combined, but compromise is her Achilles' heel.

We Christians living through the era of the Advancement no longer have the luxury of a majority consensus in Western society. We can no longer rely upon civil authority to defend us or to protect our religious rights (so hard to come by, so easy to lose). Yet our destiny as a people is, as it has always been, in the providence of God.

CHAPTER I

THE WORLDVIEW
OF THE ADVANCEMENT

SOME PEOPLE THINK that philosophical ideas are abstract and irrelevant. Some are. Nevertheless, ideas shape history and culture. Some ideas have been so profoundly influential that eras (particularly in Western civilization) can be classified by them.

All historians recognize the Middle Ages as an era of fascinating diversity, yet it is easily classified (and thus recognized) by certain unifying ideas. Likewise the Renaissance and the Enlightenment! No one should suppose that these eras had sharp chronological limits, as if they began or ended on certain days, but common ideas gradually surfaced. Often these ideas appear first in the minds of leading writers (scientists, philosophers, and theologians). Through the philosophical elite, these ideas spread in the universities (or, earlier, through the monasteries), and then through the arts to the general culture. These ideas and their collective influence form the intellectual models (the worldviews) by which individual facts and events in past centuries are interpreted.

Whereas the intellectual life of Medieval Europe was dominated by Platonic philosophy[1] and by belief in God as interpreted by the Roman Catholic Church, the intellectual life of the Renaissance was less abstract and more humanistic. It reemphasized classical Aristotelian forms and ideas.[2] The eighteenth-century Enlightenment was characterized by a decisive shift toward a more secularized form of theology, with the emphasis in theological literature turning toward ethics and religious experience. This was in some ways a reaction to the rapid developments in science that seemed to challenge the theological systems that had so closely aligned themselves with the older Aristotelian scientific assumptions. The influence of Kant and Schleiermacher can be seen in the shift away from accepting the objective teaching of Scripture as being the very Word of God toward a more subjective theology of personal experience and personal opinion.

The Modern Worldview

In the nineteenth century the Enlightenment's emphasis on morality and religious feelings continued and grew, but to this was added a sense of natural historical development and inevitable progress. Every area of life seemed to be affected by the growing secularism of the age. Individual freedom became a high priority (unless someone exercised their freedom in a way that violated another's inalienable right to freedom). But this new, secular freedom ultimately refused to submit even to God, and thus it destroyed the only possible basis for guaranteeing rights and values and freedom.[3]

Nineteenth-century concepts can be seen as forming the axioms and assumptions of "recent modern" man and, in fact, are the keys for unlocking the modern mind.[4] With many new discoveries, many previous scientific theories have had to be modified, but nineteenth-century philosophical ideas still make up much of the distinctive worldview of the so-called modern and postmodern eras. Some believe and proclaim the ideas of evolutionary progress and anti-supernaturalism; others reject and/or criticize those ideas; still others suppose that some mixture of old and new ideas is the correct perspective. Nevertheless, the nineteenth-century secularization of science and history sets the agenda and the pattern for modern thought.

The Christian Worldview

The new features of the modern worldview (natural historical development and inevitable progress) are not necessarily two absolutely distinct ideas. They are usually seen more as a blend, and it is precisely this blend that lies behind modern secular thought. In order to see the impact this blend of ideas has made, it will be helpful to contrast the modern secular and naturalistic worldview that had arisen by the late twentieth century with the idea blend (the worldview) which (in the West, at least) has been secularism's primary rival. This long-standing alternative includes the following ideas: (1) stability in nature, (2) spiritual warfare, and (3) historical change initiated by divine intervention.

This latter set of ideas more or less characterized Christian civilization prior to the nineteenth century, and it has maintained a strong following among Christian philosophers throughout the last two centuries (nineteenth and twentieth). For example, the idea of stability in nature grew out of the biblical teaching about creation. God made everything, saw that it was good, and finished his work of creation (the origination of new kinds of things) on the sixth day (cf. Gen. 1). Animals and plants were thereafter to reproduce "after their kind." This did not mean that variation and adaptation could not occur within the established limits of the biblical "kind," but it did mean that nature was understood as being basically stable. There was order and predictable regularity. This notion, in fact, was an essential element in the worldview that actually nurtured the birth of modern science.

Early modern science (1500–1750) came into being only partially because of new inventions such as the telescope. These instruments were important, but of at least equal importance were the philosophical ideas that supported the discovery of objective truth. Aristotle correctly moved away from a strict rationalism, such as might have been supported by Plato, and emphasized the unity of, for example, math, physics, and biology. Aristotle, however, never exceeded the limits of his own perceptions.

Aristotle believed in the perfection and the unchangeableness of the heavens. That is how they appeared to him. The medieval science that grew out of this Aristotelian notion concluded that the pure fire of the stars was either attached to a revolving, celestial sphere or that the stars were windows by which the pure fire showed through from the glorious realm beyond the pure crystal dome of the night sky. The heavenly perfection of the sun, and of the moon and of each known planet, was also affirmed, each one being given its own revolving sphere of pure transparent crystal.[5]

Aristotle taught that an object's natural state was to be at rest. Thus, motion proved the existence of a "mover," and for Aquinas, though not for Aristotle, the unmoved mover of all things was the biblical God. At this point Aristotle's physics and Aquinas' apologetic assumed the earth to be an unmoving fixed point in the universe; in fact, the earth was the center point of all the universal circles. Thus the rational significance of the earth was without parallel.[6]

Aristotle's medieval followers denied (before and without looking) the possibility of a blemished sun (sun spots), and they could offer no natural explanation for a comet (How did it get through the crystal spheres without breaking them?) or for a nova (stars were supposedly in a state of static perfection). The discovery of such phenomena in Galileo's day threatened Aristotle's science and church traditions, though not the Bible. Alchemy and other medieval "science projects" were also based on incorrect ancient Greek notions about the elemental makeup of the world.

Stability

Christianity[7] allows for rational order without a necessary commitment to Aristotle's physics, and thus modern science could thrive within such a cultural consensus. If God created the world, as the

Christian Bible said that he did, then the world of nature should be reasonably stable, orderly, and predictable. God was not capricious or haphazard in his work of creation or preservation. He was a personal, rational, intelligent being, and he acted with purpose.

Since mankind was made in the image of God, the universe created by God should be able to be studied and understood by men, and physical, natural truths could be experimentally discovered. If things were created, then in some sense those things must be a reflection of the mind that created them. If human minds were in some ways like the mind of the Creator, then human minds could, within the limits of that similarity, recognize and understand the created order.

If the mathematics and the observations make more sense if one assumes that planetary motion centers upon—or as Copernicus actually thought, it centers upon some point near—the sun rather than upon the earth, then those more successful, rational calculations should be accepted as being closer to the truth than the older, less successful theories. Thus Galileo argued, and nothing in the actual teaching of the Bible contradicted this approach.[8]

Some misunderstand the descriptive, observational, phenomenological language style of the Bible. They sometimes mistakenly take a phenomenologically descriptive phrase as if it were describing things from God's viewpoint rather than, as is actually the case, from the viewpoint of the human writer.[9] The clue that Holy Scripture is written from the viewpoint of individual human observers, who are always located at some geographical point, is found in Genesis 1 where the writer speaks of an "evening and a morning" as being the means of counting days, periods of light contrasted with darkness. Such descriptions are not from a vantage point somewhere out in space. "Evening and morning" is from a human observer's specific geographical point of view, and this is the way the biblical text reads even before there were any actual human observers in existence.[10]

Such is the language style of the Bible. If the Roman Curia had been less committed to Aristotle's perceptual theory of truth and more aware of this biblical language style, Galileo might not have been the center of such an unfortunate controversy between science and the church.[11] His views might have been considered more objectively and judged on their merits.

For Galileo biblical stability remained a characteristic of the world established by God. His theories in no way denied the order and scientific predictability of the world; rather, they depended on them.

Change

Order and stability—regularity—are characteristics of rationality. A rational God created the world. Thus, order and stability were assumed and sought by theists in scientific research. The world was believed by Newton and others to be what it has always been, the product of the creative action of a rational God.[12] All animals reproduced after their own kind, as did all plants. Biological variation, in the minds of the theologians, simply served to fill out God's great chain of being.[13] And life as it was now observed could be traced in its ancestry directly back to the creative hand of God. Such beliefs were held virtually by universal consent in prenineteenth-century scientific circles in Britain and in Europe.

Fossils were not unknown prior to the nineteenth century, but they were not particularly considered to be historically significant. Most fossils were thought to be the remains of older variations of the same kinds of animals that were still in existence. Extinction, not evolution, was the explanation when no similar contemporary animals were found.

Fossils were thought to have been placed on mountaintops perhaps by the biblical flood, but they were not taken as evidence of any radical changes in nature as a system. The flood surely would have brought about vast geological changes on the earth's surface, but this was clearly a historical change initiated by God.

According to the biblical record, God had initiated several historical changes since creation. Just as there was one language before Babel, and Law before Gospel, so there was the antediluvian world and the postdiluvian world. Perhaps there were other significant, divinely initiated changes that would have an effect on scientific studies—for example, in geology or in historical studies—but the underlying principle upon which even *catastrophist theory* was built was that all real, significant, and substantial change had a supernatural initiation (divine creation or divine judgment). *Nature itself, however, was thought to have remained essentially constant as a system, fixed, stable, and orderly since the beginning.*

Natural law was seen as more reliable than any man-made machine. To study the present *was* to study the past because it was assumed that nature had remained stable since the first Sabbath, the seventh day of creation.

The exception to this general rule was that modern observers would, of course, by necessity be focused on the effects of divine judgments, such as the Genesis flood, and the present was in that sense unlike the beginning. A similar distinction was made between the pre- and post-fall world. The earth currently suffers under a curse of death and decay that would not have been an original feature of the world. This would affect biology and geology and other areas of science, but regularity and stability were nevertheless crucial for scientific studies, even with these qualifications.

Spiritual Warfare

The common understanding in the premodern era of human life and human history was that though it took place in a physically stable environment, human beings were engaged in constant spiritual warfare. Satan and God were doing battle, and the battleground was the human mind; the price was the human soul.

According to the Bible, mankind had been created perfect, mentally keen, disease free, righteous—or at least innocent—and spiritually minded. Nevertheless, Adam was tempted by Satan, and Adam sinned by choosing to disobey God. Every person faces and fails a similar test, and the battle with temptation and sin is continual. The struggle of life in Western society was not primarily the physical struggle; it was the spiritual one. Judgment, and thus major historical change, came about when humanity failed in the spiritual battle. Blessing, revival, and, thus again, major historical change came about as men and women responded to the grace of God.[14]

The New Worldview

Prior to the Renaissance—actually prior to Kant—almost no one believed in gradual, inevitable progress in human history. Progress came as a gift of God when there was a turning in faith to him. Human history was primarily, however, a history of failure and judgment, broken by spiritual awakenings from time to time.

This worldview was challenged by the humanism of the Renaissance, and it was finally replaced in the nineteenth century by a modern worldview stressing gradual, inevitably progressive development and advancement in human history and in natural history. This shift is perfectly clear as far as seeing that it took place. It is, however, far from clear in the sense of seeking the authentic sources of the change.

Obviously, the intellectual roots of the modern view go back at least into the Enlightenment. Kant's view of history as progressing from the "dark" past to the intellectual "clearing up"[15] of his day was surely a major factor. Hegel proposed perhaps the most sophisticated philosophical expression of the historical development toward freedom, but "inevitable progress" became the subconscious reality of modern thinkers, whether they had ever read Hegel or Kant.

Notice the contrasts these two worldviews produce in the interpretation of nature, history, and mankind. (See table 1.) In the earlier view there is a natural stability in both history and in nature.
Progress or decline are products of a person's relationship or lack of
relationship to God, and neither is inevitable historically. To the
modern mind, however, progress is inevitable. It is a characteristic of
nature and a characteristic of mankind.[16]

Some modern theists describe reality as if it were a society. God is
preeminent but not totally controlling. Progress is inevitable because
God is active rather than static. He is a creative participant in the
community of interacting beings.[17] Some who advocate this so-
called process theology believe that God himself is dynamically
growing. The world is thought of as his body through which
he interacts with and leads the community of life. God is thought
to be the process of life itself, and thus the supposed evidence for
evolutionary change is taken as evidence for an inevitable process of
divine growth.

Table 1

	Modern View	Earlier View
Nature	naturally evolved	divinely created
	characterized by progressive development	stability of species
	transmutation of species	each kind of life distinct
	all kinds of life physically related	
	produces man's character	reflects God's character
History	physical struggle	spiritual struggle
	change natural and inevitable	change by divine intervention
	survival of the fittest	survival of the faithful
Mankind	pinnacle of biological evolution	unique creation of God
	exclusively related to animals	made in God's image
	characterized by spiritual progress	characterized by spiritual failure

Perhaps it is a characteristic of God to develop and to increase in knowledge. Perhaps God even adds to his own being by actualizing potential realities. Thus, modern thinking not only alters the earlier views of nature, history, and mankind, but it has radically changed its concept of ultimate reality. God himself has now become identified with evolutionary progress and development.[18] For modern thinkers even God is not unchanging and fixed in his nature or in his character.

Modern theologians, therefore, face problems that never occurred to their ancestors. Not only do they struggle to classify and interpret the factual data of biblical history, but they must now ask how an ancient historical event, such as the death of Christ, could have any modern significance at all. This is a major problem for them, of course, because what gave significance to such an event in traditional theology is no longer relevant to those who live inside the modern worldview. In a stable world experiencing spiritual warfare, a supreme spiritual victory is eternally significant. In a world of physical struggle and perpetual advancement, however, a victory over evil in the past might be interpreted as a major step forward in the overall pattern of spiritual advancement, but it would never settle anything in an eternal sense.

Thus, the *quest to discover and explain the significance of Christ has become a major theme of modern theology.* Some see Jesus as the outstanding example of a man properly related to God. Others give him acclaim as the true revolutionary theologian. Some find his uniqueness in his moral example or in his religious consciousness. To see him as an incarnate deity is considered by the modern mind to be a mythological belief.[19] Not all modern theologians are ready to declare incarnational Christology a myth,[20] of course, but many do, and those who do are clearly and consistently following the logic of the modern worldview to its unfortunate, though natural, conclusion.

Authentic Christianity need not fear modern thought any more than it fears heresy in general. The apostles clearly warned that in the latter days many would deny the truth and heap unto themselves teachers who would scoff at our most holy faith (cf. Jude 17–19; 2 Pet. 3:3; 2 Tim. 3:1; 4:3–4; 1 John 4:1). The truth, however, will ultimately prevail.

The older worldview is not true because it's old, and it too may be in need of refinement in light of better understandings of the Bible, but authentic Christianity is the best antidote for a culture that is dying from the venom of the Advancement. The modern world is full of good, but there are also within it some poisons—the loss of truth, the determinism of evolutionary naturalism, the inevitability of moral decay, and the absence of meaning. For all of these things and more, Christ is the answer.

CHAPTER 2

THE RISE OF ADVANCEMENT SCIENCE

IN 1543, COPERNICUS CHANGED the world with his book *De Revolutionibus*. Though the Roman Church, by way of Aristotle and Ptolemy, taught otherwise, Copernicus said that it was consistent with his measurements to conceive of the earth as not being the physical center of the universe. In fact, the earth likely was only one of several planets which revolved around the sun, or as Copernicus himself actually thought, some point near the sun. The negative reaction of the Catholic Church to these new ideas has in popular history been exaggerated, but church leaders did believe that Copernicus was wrong. It must be remembered, however, that Copernicus was a devout believer in God and in the Bible, as was Galileo.

Many scholars have recognized that the scientific revolution which developed in the sixteenth century rested on a Christian foundation.[1] The early scientists of the sixteenth and seventeenth centuries in particular believed that the scientific method—observation, experiment, and logic—could give them reliable information about the world and about the universe because the God who made their minds had made the world. There was intellectual common ground. Furthermore, the biblical God was a purposeful being, and thus one could with confidence expect to find regularity, order, and patterns in the natural world.

Because of their biblical, theistic faith, these early scientists did not believe that the scientific method described a "closed system" of reality. The natural universe was open to supernatural influences. God could intervene and change the natural order of things if he so chose. Miracles were still possible and were to be expected if God's purposes could be best served in that way. Miracles were rare, however, because God's created order (expressed through natural law) was good (cf. Gen. 1). Its weaknesses were due to the effects of the fall, not due to any inherent problem in creation itself.

Scientists in the sixteenth and seventeenth centuries generally believed that God was outside of the cause-and-effect pattern discernible in the universe. According to the Bible, mankind was created in God's image. Therefore, humankind was also in some sense outside the cause-and-effect system. Physically people lived and worked in the world, but in their essential nature they were in the likeness of a personal God. An individual, of course, did not have the power that God possessed, but people were believed to be active choosing agents who could affect their own destiny. The universal cause-and-effect system of nature could influence the human body, and it controlled the environment, but it did not dominate the person. The human mind was not trapped by natural cause-and-effect patterns.

The universe was believed to be regular and orderly because it was created by a God who is a rational being. God had created the universe according to his own specific, clear, rational pattern. People could think clearly and logically because God had given them a rational mind. Since the rationality of the human mind and the orderliness of the universe came from the same source, it was to be expected that a human mind could understand and adequately approach the proper interpretation of the natural universe.

However, scientific research did not always continue its development within this theistic framework. Many scientists continued to use the word *God*, but the concept of God was slowly pushed out of their systems of explanation. In the eighteenth and nineteenth centuries, it became the accepted norm and the standard practice to explain features of the universe without reference to their Creator at all.

Many today share a common opinion that any direct reference to a Creator—or even an indirect reference, such as a reference to teleological purpose in nature—is ipso facto a nonscientific explanation. Nothing is thought of as being outside the natural cause-and-effect system. Humanity itself is thought to be simply a product of chance and natural causes. Everything is seen as a part of one vast impersonal system.

The first noticeable symptoms of this shift from a Christian to a naturalistic worldview within the church began to show up among the eighteenth-century Deists. God had created everything, they said, but God simply left the universe to run by its own natural powers. God was seen as the originator of the natural laws, but there was no emphasis on God as their providential upholder. Natural law had not yet become autonomous in the eighteenth century, but the die had been cast. For Deists, God was transcendent, but he was not imminent.

Like so many compromise theories, however, the deistic view is internally inconsistent and, thus, unstable. It is arbitrary to believe in a Creator and then relegate him to a position of no imminent power. Deism is a compromise that settles nothing and thus makes God irrelevant. Conservative theologians correctly perceived Deism as a heretical liberalism, and naturalistic philosophers and scientists saw no reason to give up their naturalism, even at a supposed beginning point.

The Philosophy of Science

The idea that reality could be explained by pure cause-and-effect reasoning was first applied to physics, chemistry, and astronomy.[2] Today, however, the cause-and-effect theory has been applied to sociology, psychology, economics, history, and even religious studies. This new viewpoint did not come about because the scientists discovered new data which forced them to this position. No data has demonstrated that God did not create the world or that God cannot perform miracles. The issue is not data but presuppositions. The concept that strictly natural cause-and-effect explanations must apply to every academic discipline did not come from that which could be demonstrated by science, but it did come from the success and the influence of those who successfully interpreted the data in their fields from this new secular, philosophical base.

The Bible clearly teaches that God created the universe and that he has uniquely fashioned the earth as a dwelling place for mankind. Scripture also provides a historical record of mankind's fall into sin and of God's redemptive acts (some of which were miraculous). Valid belief in creation is not a denial of any of the scientific facts. However, to affirm biblical creation is to challenge naturalistic presuppositions. Acknowledgment of the validity of biblical history also challenges the naturalistic philosophy of science that is so characteristic of the advancement.

When key scientists, especially in the eighteenth and nineteenth centuries, gave up their belief in God and began to interpret the scientific data on naturalistic or materialistic assumptions, they found that it was possible to construct a fairly comprehensive interpretation of the data in that way. Those proposing these ideas did so with great sophistication. As Scripture itself acknowledges, sinful people are naturally set against God and against God's truth. Scientific explanations which did not remind people of God or thrust moral implications upon the hearer were more likely to be accepted by the increasingly secular general public than those more teleological scientific interpretations which did relate all things to God's will and purpose.

Modern Materialism

Materialistic ideas continued to grow until they reached a climax in the nineteenth century. In 1899, Ernst Haeckel wrote a book entitled *The Riddle of the Universe at the Close of the Nineteenth Century*. This book became a best-seller and was influential among both scientists and laymen. In the book he suggested that matter and energy are eternal. All things, including the human mind, were to be explained on a truly materialistic cause-and-effect basis. Such explanations, he believed, would solve the riddle of the universe.

In his famous two-volume work *The History of Creation: Or the Development of the Earth and Its Inhabitants by the Action of Natural Causes* (1884), Haeckel writes:

The great value of the Theory of Descent in regard to Biology consists, as I have already remarked, in its explaining to us the origin of organic forms in a mechanical way, and pointing out their active causes. But however highly and justly this service of the Theory of Descent may be valued, yet it is almost eclipsed by the immense importance which a single necessary inference from it claims for itself alone. This necessary and unavoidable inference is the theory of the *animal descent of the human race*.

The determination of the position of man in nature, and of his relations to the totality of things—this question of all questions for mankind, as Huxley justly calls it—is finally solved by the knowledge that man is descended from animals. In consequence of Darwin's reformed Theory of Descent, we are now in a position to establish scientifically the ground work of a *non-miraculous history of the development of the human race*. All those who have defended Darwin's theory as well as all its thoughtful opponents, have acknowledged that, as a matter of necessity, it followed from his theory that the human race, in the first place, must be traced to ape-like animals. . . . Manifestly the effect of this conclusion is immense, and *no* science will be able to escape from the consequences.

If we understand the creation to mean the *coming into existence of a body* by a creative power or force, we may then either think of the *coming into existence of its substance* (corporeal matter), or of the *coming into existence of its form* (the corporeal form).

Creation in the former sense, as the *coming into existence of matter,* does not concern us here at all. This process, if indeed it ever took place, is completely beyond human comprehension, and can therefore never become a subject of scientific inquiry. Natural science teaches that matter is eternal and imperishable, for experience has never shown us that even the smallest particle of matter has come into existence or passed away. Where a natural body seems to disappear, as for example by burning, decaying, evaporation, etc., it merely changes its form, its physical composition or chemical combination. In like manner the coming into existence of a natural body, upon the different particles, which had before existed in a certain form or combination, assuming a new form or combination in consequence of changed conditions of existence. But never yet has an instance been observed of even the smallest particle of matter having vanished, or even of an atom being added to the already existing mass. Hence a naturalist can no more imagine the coming into existence of matter, than he can imagine its disappearance, and he therefore looks upon the existing quantity matter in the universe as a given fact. If any person feels the necessity of conceiving the coming into existence of this matter as the work of a supernatural creative power, of the creative force of something outside of matter, we have nothing to say against it. But we must remark, that thereby not even the smallest advantage is gained for a scientific knowledge of nature. Such a conception of an immaterial force, which at the first creates matter, is an article of faith which has nothing whatever to do with human science. *Where faith commences, science ends.* Both these arts of the human mind must be strictly kept apart from each other. Faith has its origin in the poetic imagination; knowledge, on the other hand, originates in the reasoning intelligence of man. Science has to pluck the best fruits from the tree of knowledge, unconcerned whether these consequences trench upon the poetical imagination of faith or not.

If, therefore, science makes the "history of creation" its highest, most difficult, and most comprehensive problem, it must accept as its idea of creation the second explanation of the word, viz. *the coming into being of the form* of natural bodies. In this way, geology, which tries to investigate the origin of the inorganic surface of the earth as it now appears, and the manifold historical changes in the form of the solid crust of the earth, may be called the history of the creation of the earth. In like manner, the history of the development of animals and plants, which investigates the origin of living forms, and the manifold historical changes in animal and vegetable forms, may be termed the history of the creation of organisms. As, however, in the idea of creation, although used in this sense, the unscientific idea of a creator existing outside of matter, and changing it, may easily creep in, it will perhaps be better in future to substitute for it the more accurate term, *development.*[3]

As this way of thinking became dominant within twentieth-century Western civilization, in effect, God died. But if God dies, then man, who is made in his image, also dies. Man is no longer a unique personality purposefully created; he is the accidental result of a complicated process. People become simply a part of the machine.

The Rise of Uniformitarian Thought

Every scientific discipline has moved rapidly toward a materialistic interpretation of reality. The first major study of geology from the modern materialistic viewpoint was James Hutton's *Theory of the Earth* (1795). In direct contrast to the prevailing view of earlier geologists, Hutton believed that the earth had never experienced any major geologically significant catastrophes. The mountains, he suggested, had been uplifted at a rate of only millimeters per millennia. He did not believe that the earth had ever been shaped or formed by any miraculous act of God, such as a worldwide flood, whether in Noah's day or at any other time. Nor did he believe it had ever been significantly changed in a naturally rapid manner.

His basic evidence was simply his contemporary experience. Hutton was aware of local catastrophes, of course—floods or earthquakes or volcanoes that did shape the face of the earth in local areas—but he believed that what he could see in his experience—gradual erosion; tides; rain; wind; slow, almost imperceptible changes in the landscape—must be the universal and everlasting method of general change in earth history. The assumption that currently observable processes must be uniformly applied to the geological history of the earth is known as uniformitarianism.

Hutton's work was rejected at first by traditional geologists who generally assumed that at least one geologically significant catastrophe had shaped the earth because Scripture, and many other ancient traditions, recorded the history of a massive flood. The vast quantities of sedimentary materials in the earth's crust seemed consistent with the fact of such a flood; the great canyons of the earth seemed to have been dug rapidly by huge amounts of water, and the earth was not believed to be old enough to explain everything in terms of gradual processes. Nevertheless, the growing influence of nontheistic materialism made Hutton's views attractive to some. His actual theories were not based on significant research, however, and they could not really be said to be scientifically credible at that time.

A more serious scientific theory, however, was proposed by Charles Lyell in his multivolume work, *Principles of Geology* (1830–1833). He countered the generally accepted catastrophic theories of earth history by suggesting an extended geological time scale for every geological event, because God was stable and consistent. Lyell's theories were not widely accepted at first, primarily because they opposed many of the generally accepted religious and scientific ideas about a relatively short earth history. Most scientists in Lyell's day still assumed that God had created the earth, that he had at one time destroyed it with a geologically universal flood, and that the Bible taught a relatively recent date for creation itself. Lyell, however, was a religious man himself. He strongly affirmed his Christian faith, and he never came to accept Darwin's evolutionary theories. He did believe the earth was ancient, however, because God was ancient.

One interesting sidelight,[4] which illustrates the changing attitudes toward the length of time involved in earth's history, relates to Lyell's dating of the most recent ice age—assuming for the moment, without argument, the widely held belief in multiple ice ages, though the illustration does not depend on that form of the theory. At first he dated that last ice age about 1,000,000 B.C. It had come about, he suggested, by the slow accumulation of snowflakes descending over long periods of time. There are geological ways of measuring time, however, and one of those ways relates specifically to this ice age.

Apparently Lake Ontario was formed near the end of the most recent ice age. Between Lake Erie and Lake Ontario is a crystalline formation which is being eroded by Niagara Falls. This erosion is taking place at a measurable rate. By measuring the distance of the Falls from their supposed original location at Lake Ontario, it would seem that one could calculate the length of time this erosion had been taking place. The Falls are receding from Lake Ontario toward Lake Erie.

By interviewing the inhabitants of the area, Lyell discovered that the rate of erosion was perhaps three feet every year. This, of course, was impossible, according to Lyell. If the rate were three feet per year, the Falls could have reached their current location in only twelve thousand years. That would mean that Niagara Falls would not have begun to recede from the newly formed Lake Ontario until some 988,000 years after Lyell's suggested date for the most recent ice age. This seemed obviously impossible, so Lyell concluded that the local residents must have been greatly exaggerating the rate of erosion. He revised his observational evidence and concluded that the rate of erosion was perhaps one foot per year rather than three. This still demanded a revision of his original estimate of the date of the ice age. So he finally concluded, albeit reluctantly, that the most recent ice epoch, which formed Lake Ontario, had ended around 35,000 B.C.

According to some scholars, Niagara Falls today has been naturally retreating from Lake Ontario at a rate approaching five feet per year. The erosion rate has been so rapid that to preserve their tourist value and to develop a complex waterway with vast hydroelectric capabilities, some work has been done by the U.S. Army Corps of Engineers in recent years to halt, or at least greatly retard, the rapid erosion process. The erosion rate immediately after the ice age would perhaps have been even more rapid than it is today.

This one example certainly does not totally discredit Lyell's work, but it does indicate his attitude toward time as it related to earth history. His theories of gradual change, uniformitarian geology, demanded enormous amounts of time. His tendency seems to have been to give himself the benefit of every doubt. Therefore, he moved the age of geological events as far back in earth history as he could conceivably move them.

The Rise of an Evolutionary Worldview

The natural sciences did not immediately accept Lyell's theories; however, the more humanistically oriented social sciences did welcome them. Charles Darwin's famous book, *The Origin of Species by Means of Natural Selection* (1859), proposed a biological theory that was in many ways parallel to Lyell's geological theory.[5] Darwin, too, was strongly opposed at first by many in the scientific community as well as in the religious community.[6] However, his book became a best-seller among the general public. The entire first edition sold out the first day the book went on the market.

Both Lyell and Darwin offered scientific suggestions that were in keeping with the growing materialistic assumptions of Western society. Mathematical studies of the probability factors involved—perhaps *improbability factors* would be a better term—indicate that random chance could not have produced the complexity known to exist in modern biological systems in any amount of time currently being suggested even for the age of the universe.[7] If one starts with a big bang explosion, then one must start either with utter chaos or utter simplicity or both. To get from a random expansion of simple hydrogen atoms, assuming they could have been spontaneously produced, to the known complexity of modern biological systems by a nondirected, chance-driven process in the several billions of years which are available, according to current scientific estimates, would be a feat nothing short of the miraculous. What modern secular scientists believe is far more incredible than any biblical miracle accepted by the simple Christian believer.

Evolution and Ethics

Herbert Spencer (1820–1903), an English philosopher from Derby, despite his lack of formal education, conceived the idea of bringing together under one scheme all the scientific knowledge of his day. He exalted the individual over society and science over religion. In 1860, Spencer prepared a prospectus and arranged financing, by donations, to produce a true synthetic philosophy. A prolific writer, Spencer took his new philosophical theory of evolution and set it forth in his *First Principles* (1862; rev. ed. 1900) and then applied it in his *Principles of Biology* (2 vols., 1864–1867; rev. ed. 1898–1899), *Principles of Sociology* (3 vols., 1876–1896), *Principles of Ethics* (2 vols., 1892–1893), and *Principles of Psychology* (2 vols., 1855, 1872; 4th ed., 1899).

The great law of nature, as he saw it, was the constant interaction of forces resulting in a natural development from simple to complex. Spencer believed that the human mind had developed by such a process, moving from the simple automatic reactions of animals to the rational processes of human beings. Individuals gain particular, specific bits of knowledge, but there is also an intuitive knowledge that is learned unconsciously. This, he claimed, was the inherited knowledge or the collective experience of the human race. (Spencer is often cited as the great exponent of Victorian optimism.)

Nevertheless, an opposing force that Spencer called dissolution tends to destroy complexity and return things to simpler forms. Progress occurs when evolution is stronger than dissolution. Spencer's theory in this form could be and was applied to every aspect of life. It should be remembered, however, that many of Spencer's scientific ideas were later discredited. His philosophical ideas, nevertheless, continued to influence the general public.

Spencer coined the phrase "survival of the fittest" to describe Darwin's theory of "natural selection," itself a rather anthropomorphic misnomer. The idea seemed to catch on, and in only a few years the theory of biological evolution had become a theory of universal natural evolution. What at first had been strictly a theory of the origin of species had now become a philosophical basis for all of life.

The capitalistic economy of the West was ready-made to support such ideas. Poverty became the sign of inherent inferiority. The strong began to use evolutionary philosophy to justify whatever was necessary to achieve their goals of political, social, and economic power. The Christian notion of charity and self-giving was increasingly replaced by an ethic of strength over weakness.

Marxist economics also adopted the evolutionary ethic. Struggle was seen as being essential to progress, and individual values were pushed aside for the good of the collective state, the communist commonwealth. The Nazi movement in Germany was one of the logical conclusions of these ideas. For some people racism was scientifically justified on evolutionary biological grounds.

The influence of evolutionary theories became so pervasive in the twentieth century that it is almost impossible for some people today to think biblically about these matters. As an illustration, the Bible never distinguishes men on the basis of their race. In fact, the Bible does not distinguish between the races of mankind. It does make distinctions on the basis of religion, nationality, language, and other tribal differences, but consistently the Bible argues that all people are of one blood and that all humans are one race, the human race, mankind created in the image of God.

All modern people descended not from animals (the so-called common ancestors) but from Adam (the common, historic, human ancestor of all people). Through his sin, death came upon all of us. Jesus was nationally and religiously a Jew, but his atonement was equally available to all nationalities, because he is one with all people in his human nature. Christ is the second Adam.

Paul makes a distinction between the flesh of mankind and the flesh of animals, but he does not make a distinction between the flesh of one man and the flesh of another man. Social and religious customs separate people one from another, but in Christ there is no division. The Darwinian/Spenserian theories of evolution have so infiltrated the minds of modern thinkers that many of them can no longer hear this biblical word. Only by the power of the Holy Spirit can any of us hear and understand God's truth.

Some of the most crucial issues of the modern day come from the continuing developments in the biological sciences. Philosophical naturalism simply has no basis for answering the questions that inevitably must be faced. Mankind is now capable of genetic engineering, but who has the right to decide how and who should be changed? If medical costs continue to rise, will the strong—the wealthy—conclude that it is economically unsound to keep the weak alive? Can abortion be justified on the grounds that a woman has the right to control her own body and thus that she has the right to remove from her body a living being who is temporarily living in a state of total dependency upon her? Is the day far off when some will suggest, and get political support for the idea, that birth control measures should be required of certain segments of society which are considered to be weak and unprofitable? Will clones belong to their creators? Do genetic codes eliminate human freedom? These issues and a thousand others grow directly out of the modern loss of the biblical concepts concerning creation and the unique significance and value of human life.

Many Christians have tried to develop compromise positions by which they hope to be able to maintain their theistic commitments and yet accept the interpretations of biological data which are provided by the secular humanists. The desire to be accepted by one's peer group is strong, and many Christians believe that at least some elements of the evolutionary hypothesis are descriptively true of the way God did it.

This is not an area for shallow thinking. Christians must become informed about the nature of the evidence, about the implications of the various viewpoints, and about the viable alternatives within the framework of a recognition that the Bible is the normative source of truth about God and about man.

The Disappearance of Humanness

As suggested earlier, the work of Copernicus produced a revolution in cosmology. His work seemed to attack theological doctrines because it removed earth from the center of the universe. However, it was soon realized, and properly so, that the earth did not have to be the physical center of the universe in order to be affirmed as the spiritual center of the universe. This solution does not violate any proper approach to biblical exegesis.

Scripture does not claim or teach anything about earth's physical location in the universe. All supposed claims of this type are due to the characteristic phenomonenological language of appearance that the Bible uses. The Bible says nothing explicitly about earth's being the spiritual center of the universe. The Bible says God created the heavens and the earth, and then it proceeds to describe God's activity from an earthly point of view. Earth is surely a special place because here God made human beings in his own image. Here God acted redemptively, revealed himself in incarnate form, gave his only Son as an atonement for sin, and promised to return personally to restore all things and thus to dwell with his people forever. Since Christ was God's only Son, earth must be special, even unique, but Scripture gives us no clue about God's relationship to other parts of the universe, and thus it is speculative to speak of earth as the center of God's infinite attention or of his universe. Clearly it is temporary, for the Bible describes a new earth that is yet to come.

By the mid-nineteenth century, however, evolutionary theories had proposed natural selection as the basic mechanism by which all life-forms had developed. This attack was not simply on the ideas about the physical location of the earth in space; it was a direct attack on mankind's special created nature. By the logical necessity of the evolutionary theory, humans were not created, but that they had simply and naturally survived because they were the most fit creatures. Evolutionary thought questioned the unique nature of mankind; it denied the existence of an original divine image and a subsequent fall into sin; it denied the biblical teaching of the special creation of mankind, and it clearly denied the biblical account of the origin of male and female.

Some theologians attempted to solve this problem by affirming that it was a man's soul, his spiritual nature, that was uniquely created. The body was a natural development of the evolutionary process. Though this answer at first glance seems to parallel the biblical interpretive approach that was taken in response to the theory of Copernicus, it was, in fact, a far more significant change, a change in biblical theology.

The shift from physical to spiritual importance for the earth itself or for the people on the earth was not a violation of sound exegesis, but the distinction between a man's body and a man's soul goes against a basic biblical teaching about human nature. The biblical emphasis is clearly on man's unity.

The human body is related to nature, and it is similar in many respects to the body of animals. Biblically speaking, God made both animals and Adam from the dust of the ground. The chemical composition and structure is similar in both, but with Adam the action was distinctively unique, deliberate, direct, and purposeful. Man was shaped in God's image and after God's likeness. Adam also had a spiritual nature. His conscious life began as God breathed into his nostrils the breath of life. That is how and when Adam became a living soul. From creation onward man as a unity of body and spirit is the concern of the biblical witness.

Eschatological bodily resurrection is promised only to Adam and his descendants, only to the uniquely created human kind. Thus Christian orthodoxy has consistently resisted Darwinian evolution, providing both theological reasons and substantial scientific evidences against evolutionary theories.

The challenge to biblical ideas from advancement philosophy has become even more serious in the twentieth century. In 1927, Sigmund Freud published *The Future of an Illusion*. Freud argued that religion is simply a belief based on wish fulfillment or wish illusion rather than on reality. In 1928, John B. Watson published *The Ways of Behaviorism*. The human mind, our spiritual nature, was now being described by leading thinkers in the scientific community purely as a natural phenomena.

No significant doctrinal implications are attached to the discovery that Earth is not located in a central stationary place in the universe. However, the claim that the human body supposedly evolved naturally was a significant move away from biblical teachings. A few short steps and mankind's mental ability was seen as a product of impersonal natural forces. Men and women no longer are what men and women have always been thought to be. Humans are no longer human. They are simply naked apes, complex conglomerations of carbon compounds, sophisticated bits of protoplasm, products of chemical reactions in ancient supernovas, marvelous stimulus-response mechanisms, highly adaptive creatures but not humans created by direct divine activity, not male and female in the image of God.

The challenges to faith today are no longer couched simply in terms of the older creationist-evolutionist debates, though the seeming victory of evolution is one direct cause of these contemporary challenges. The question today is whether a person can still be thought of as human at all! According to some, even our deepest spiritual insights are strictly stimulus-response mechanisms. Man, in the biblical sense, simply does not exist according to modern naturalistic science. Only a reaffirmation of biblical creation, a valid critique of naturalistic evolutionary "science," and a reexposition of the viable, alternative, biblical views of mankind can save us from the fate that awaits any civilization that suppresses the truth of God.

Paul wrote in Romans 1:18–25:

> The wrath of God is being revealed from heaven against
> all the godlessness and wickedness of men who suppress the
> truth by their wickedness, since what may be known about
> God is plain to them, because God has made it plain to
> them. For since the creation of the world God's invisible
> qualities—his eternal power and divine nature—have been

clearly seen, being understood from what has been made, so that men are without excuse.

For although they knew God, they neither glorified him as God nor gave thanks to him, but their thinking became futile and their foolish hearts were darkened. Although they claimed to be wise, they became fools and exchanged the glory of the immortal God for images made to look like mortal man and birds and animals and reptiles.

Therefore God gave them over in the sinful desires of their hearts to sexual impurity for the degrading of their bodies with one another. They exchanged the truth of God for a lie, and worshiped and served created things rather than the Creator—who is forever praised. Amen.

CHAPTER 3

THE ADVANCEMENT AND THE
THEORY OF KNOWLEDGE

ONE CRUCIAL ELEMENT of modern thought, often overlooked, is the shift in epistemology[1] that came with and supported the modern worldview. This foundational change is perhaps most clearly seen in the context of scientific research.

According to the earlier, more biblical view, mankind was created in the image of the God who created us. This image surely refers to several things about human beings, but apparently it has a special reference to mankind's spiritual nature and our ability to communicate with and respond to God. Such a spiritual nature, however, requires an extremely complex mental ability, one capable of meaningful language and rational insight. Human beings were believed to be able to think and communicate with one another and with God in patterns somewhat similar to the rational patterns of God's creative actions.

Thus nature, which is also a product of God's rational creative actions, would be capable of being understood by a human mind, and this human understanding is possibly true. If our understanding of some particular matter is correct—that is, if the ideas out of which this understanding is composed correspond in some significant way to substantial details of the reality being studied and if the relationships between the various elements or activities of the reality being studied are properly described—then we can argue that we have truth and not error in our statements and conclusions about that particular matter.

There is, moreover, in a theistic worldview, a basis and a source for truth outside of and other than from human observation alone. Truth is often achieved through scientific (i.e., careful, systematic, directed) research, but the ground and justification for knowing truth to be truth are found in a unified, external, spiritual source. The real existence of this source, God himself, is the only viable guarantee of the objectivity of truth.[2]

Because someone believes in God does not, of course, guarantee that individual is always correct in his or her conclusions about other matters. Many factors cause or permit human error, including the obvious fact of human finiteness, not to mention prejudice, closed-mindedness, and/or a lack of intellectual humility. Nevertheless, to believe in God is at least to affirm a view that makes real truth possible. Though it is often not even considered, this principle is especially important in modern naturalistic scientific research.

Biological Evolution and Knowledge

A modern philosophical model, such as naturalistic biological evolution, faces a real crisis when it tries to justify scientific knowledge. To see that this is so, one need only reflect briefly on the basic elements of this evolutionary model of explanation.

Naturalistic biological evolution explains the variety of living things as being a set of natural variations of organic matter. Every life-form, including human life, supposedly arose from the same underlying reality. Everything is a variation of one thing, and that one thing is the matrix of space, time, matter, and energy. There is no supernatural element. There is only the basic physical reality we call nature.

Organic matter is thought of as a naturally occurring set of unusually complex chemical chains—molecules—built around the element carbon. According to the naturalistic theory, the difference between life and nonlife has to do with the complexity of these special molecules, the active chemical features of carbon, and the distinctive interactions of this specific set of organic molecules as opposed to other sets of inorganic molecules.[3] Apes and amoebas, according to this theory, are biologically linked not only by chemistry but also by a long natural cause-and-effect process of gradual change with no supernatural intervention of any kind. Variation within organic life-forms arises from and through environmental pressures and fortuitous circumstances only. Moreover, organic and inorganic matter is thought ultimately to be natural variations of a single, underlying, natural matter-energy reality. All is one (monism). No transcendent reality is admitted.

If the rational human mind is merely a biological product, which it must be if naturalistic evolution were true, then the mind is not an independent observer, no matter how complex or sophisticated it may be, and it is therefore not truly free to explore or examine reality. The functions of the mind would be produced and controlled solely by the genetic, chemical makeup of and the environmental influences on each individual. Because of the complexity of the mental faculties—the brain itself being incredibly intricate—there would be some natural variation in thought patterns, so not everyone would think exactly alike, but the variations would be like the multitude of variations found in roses or in dogs. Just as Peace and American Beauty are both roses despite their significant differences, and Great Danes and Yorkshire terriers are both dogs despite their differences, so atheism and theism would simply be examples of natural variations of human thought, and one could not be more true than the other in any objective or absolute sense.

According to many who hold naturalistic evolutionary theories, theism arises in human minds from thought patterns set and determined by the initial, genetically controlled mental system as it has been shaped by positive and negative experiences that flow from environmental interactions including parental instruction, peer relationships, and cultural settings. By this theory, however, atheism must also come from exactly the same source, only having been modified by different experiences. Who is to say that they or another person is ever ultimately right or wrong about anything? All that can be said is that my genetic makeup and experiences have led me to affirm this, and your genetic makeup and experiences have led you to affirm that. When confronted with serious options with regard to some matter of concern, we try to find ways to decide whether our experiences are of sufficient quality and quantity to justify our continuing to hold a particular theory or idea.

The Dilemma

The basic problem with all of this is that a strict and necessary relativism involved here can only be resolved pragmatically. Where the pragmatic model of inquiry prevails, however, where pragmatism is the fundamental theory of knowledge, there is no longer truth as such. There is at best only warranted belief or accepted policy or majority vote, or some other pragmatic method of decision making.

If naturalism is a proper description of reality, man's mind could not be truly free to look at biological facts objectively. The human mind would exclusively be a product of the biological facts being studied. Or to be more precise, the mind and the biological facts would be products of the same underlying, nonrational, nonpurposive, chemically describable, ultimate reality. The mind would, thus, be limited by the parameters set by the physical and chemical laws and processes involved in producing the mind. The mind would not be separate and apart from the biology of the body; rather it would be a special function of that biology. Therefore it would be limited by the limits of that biology. Surely this is a vicious circle.

Do evolutionists believe in evolution because they are biologically determined and sociologically constrained by the evolutionary process to believe in evolution? Do theists believe in God and in a creation model for the same reason?

If the mind is a product only of natural forces and processes, then in what significant sense could it be said to be free to do research and to discover truth in an objective way? If rational thought is determined by unthinking, unknowing physical processes, then how could and why should it be trusted? Would there be any significance to what we call the decision-making process? Is meaning itself simply an illusion?

The Reply

The reply normally given to this basic critique of naturalistic philosophy is that, strictly by the process of evolution, the mind has finally reached a point where it has transcended itself and has now evolved to be able to understand itself. This is a self-congratulatory affirmation at best, but it is hard to imagine how one could know it was true.

The best attempt so far is to claim that science is supposedly self-correcting. In other words, a naturalist might argue that the mind does not have to be free in the theistic/creationist sense because theories are not private, and the investigative tradition of modern science serves to check and double-check on theories proposed, and only a broad consensus of authorities grants the status of truth to a theory.

But this is no solution to the epistemological dilemma of naturalism. All of the minds who check and double-check the theories are equally bound by the parameters set for them by their biological ancestors and by their subjective experiences.

Supposed agreement among reports of subjective experiences might be acceptable evidence if one had a way to know that the reports were objectively valid instead of only verbally similar, but that would require some source of knowledge other than the personal, verbal reports themselves by which to test their reliability. This, however, is exactly what naturalism does not have.[4]

Theists generally would agree that experiences contrary to a certain theory may be used in an attempt to falsify the proposed theory, but experiences meeting the expectations of the theory do not with equal justification show the theory to be true. Rather, they show the theory to be useful.

Showing something to be useful is a useful thing to do. Modern technology has in many ways been useful, so useful in fact that the traditional concern and quest for truth has simply been given up by many scientists and laymen. If a certain combination of chemicals produces a marketable product, it is of little interest to most businessmen to discuss the objective or absolute truthfulness of the atomic theory that claims to explain why such chemical combinations produce such a product. Even those who do look at it often stop looking when the mathematics of the symbolic formulas balance. New discoveries often come from intuition or occur by accident. We later attempt to explain them by standard theories, but after-the-fact explanations can be given for anything.

The one who asks where energy/matter came from will most likely be called an abstract philosopher who talks over everybody's head. Moreover, religion has no place in a science classroom: so goes the wisdom of the age.

The Result

Scientists, no less than the rest of us, often settle for a theory that works, that has predictable results, and that can be put into effect at will. Truth, as such, has become unnecessary for many modern thinkers. Ultimate reality may be indeterminate, they say, but we can still build machines that will work.

This attitude characterizes the modern secular mind. The one and only unacceptable position in modern scholarship is dogmatism, especially religious dogmatism. The one acceptable absolute is that there are no other absolutes, certainly not moral ones. The only viewpoint that is not considered worthy of discussion is one that builds itself on the premodern worldview. Thus, truth is discarded.

For example, fundamental Christian orthodoxy, characterized by the affirmation of biblical infallibility and inerrancy, is the only theological viewpoint that cannot be tolerated or listened to sympathetically by modern theologians. One reason this is so is that biblical theology, as understood by conservative theologians who allow biblical content to determine theological expression, assumes the earlier worldview and thus interprets facts in keeping with that earlier view. Their theory of knowledge is different, and thus communication between the two worldviews is difficult at best and perhaps impossible.

The real question, therefore, is not whether the theological options, biblical orthodoxy or modernism, have all their interpretations and doctrines stated correctly. (Surely there is always room for clarification, for more mature reflection, for more profound insight.) The more basic questions that must be settled are whether the modern worldview can, even in principle, ever achieve real truth scientifically or theologically and whether such truth would be worth achieving.

The Traditional Theory of Knowledge

Perhaps a diagram can help to clarify the various worldviews and their theories of knowledge. The traditional view incorporates the biblical ideas of the creation of nature and of the creation of mankind. Human beings are uniquely created in God's image though they are physically a part of nature. (See figure 1.) Mankind and nature have a common position in that both are totally dependent on God. There is no autonomous area within humanity or within nature. There is real freedom, however, which serves as the basis of moral responsibility and values, but this freedom is granted

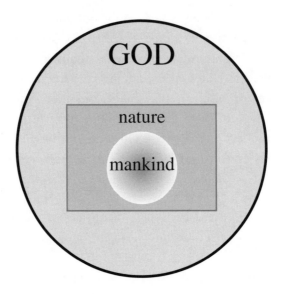

Figure 1

and guaranteed by God, not achieved by human effort or natural biological development.

Mankind's physical existence is directly linked to nature which supplies light, heat, food, air, water, and raw materials for clothing, shelter, and technological use. This is such a strong and obvious link of dependence that many ancient pagan religions centered on the worship of various elements of the physical universe. The more profound religions, however, worshiped a transcendent God who created the heavens and the earth and all that is in them.

Mankind, in the traditional worldview, is also uniquely related to God. Human beings are not simply or purely physical beings. They are spiritual beings who think, perceive, communicate, and relate to their environment at a level far superior to the other living beings of nature, such as the animals. This difference is a qualitative one of essence, not merely one of advanced physical sophistication. If we concentrate on this uniquely created aspect of mankind, it is possible to draw another type of diagram that perhaps more clearly expresses the theory of knowledge of the traditional, biblical world-view. (See figure 2.)

The human mind can directly observe and come to know nature as it is. The mind can also be told by God what nature is. It can hear and understand the Word of God and thus come to understand that nature is a created reality. People are free to study nature from every angle, and their biblical position is to serve as God's caretakers for this world. We name, classify, use, and should protect the elements of nature.

Though the human spirit or mind is truly separate from nature in its origin, it nevertheless touches nature through the physical human body. In particular, we think of the mind as being uniquely related to the brain, which is uniquely linked to all of the body's sensory apparatus. The body is exquisitely tuned for sensory data, and the brain is a wondrous processor of that data, but the body is an object limited by space, time, and physical strength. Thus, human knowledge of the world is limited by human finiteness and by the relationship between the human mind and God's revelatory Word.

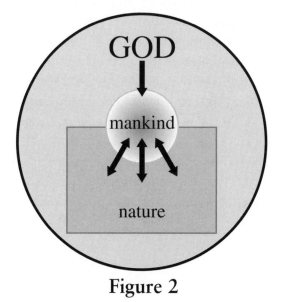

Figure 2

Sin has negative epistemological consequences. The mind is a spiritual reality characterized by intelligence and volition. This human will is the manifestation of God's gift of responsible freedom, but it is distorted by sin and may even resist the truth.

Because God created nature in its entirety, nature must in every way reflect God's creative activity. Nature is thus a product of divine, intentional activity. The similarity between God and humanity, expressed by the doctrine of mankind being made in God's image, does not come at the point of creative ability or power, but it does include mankind's ability to understand divine intention.

Humans can see and understand what God did. Humans can see and understand how and why God related the various elements of nature the way he did. Humans can learn to use these inherent qualities and relationships in nature to meet their needs and desires. What is learned may be the real truth. Though people often discover only part of the truth, real truth is a possible result of their study because real truth exists—God knows and determines what it is—and the human mind is capable of comprehending it.

The divine intention for nature and the divine understanding of nature are the absolutely true purpose for nature and the full and complete knowledge of the truth about natural reality. Mankind in God's image is potentially capable of thinking about nature as God thinks about nature. The human mind is not capable of exhaustive knowledge of all truth, but it is capable of knowing truth in both natural and supernatural realms. For humanity, moral knowledge is the most controversial, a point not overlooked by authentic Christianity. The human mind, according to the Bible, is not biologically determined; rather, it is theologically free to study, learn, and know. Sin has bound the will, and sin makes wrong look attractive, but the biblical God holds his people accountable, and ignorance is no excuse.

The Modern Theory of Knowledge

A person can in general trust his or her senses, for they were made by God. However, human reason must act to detect illusion and deception, for reason must test all sensory data to discover truth and discern error. This is not always an easy process. Thus, a rational procedure of observing, hypothetically interpreting, testing, reinter-preting, retesting, refining the hypothetical interpretation, retesting, and so on, has been found to be necessary if we are to approach the truth about the more complex aspects of reality.

This so-called scientific procedure is a legitimate recognition of our finite, human limitations. Interestingly enough, it came into widespread, formal use at that time in history when human beings were forced to recognize the vastness of the universe and thus the vastness of the data that must be considered in any comprehensive knowledge claim. This scientific method is a good procedure, and properly used it should lead people increasingly toward truth.

The modern worldview, however, has set up a new situation entirely. Perhaps a diagram can help here as well. (See figure 3.)

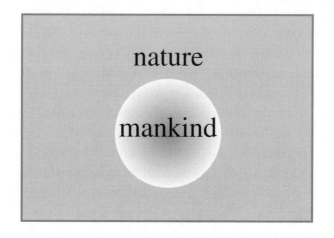

Figure 3

Mankind, according to modern thought, is seen as totally related to nature. People are thought of entirely as products of biological evolution. There is no supernatural reality at all in the modern worldview.

If God were included in figure 3, he would either be a synonym for nature or drawn as a smaller circle inside the human circle. In other words, God is seen by naturalistic modern minds as a semantic confusion. People speak of God as being "out there" when in fact only nature is "out there"—or as a psychological projection—people believe in God because they want to so badly that they make up a God in whatever imaginary form they choose. Humanity's existence is seen strictly as a product of nature's incessant activity, which in earth's fortuitous environment has been characterized by progressive, advancing change and development—what mankind is and what people think comes as the direct product of the biological processes of this fertile natural environment.

By assuming the cosmological principle, that the universe is truly isotropic—that is, that the universe is similar everywhere—we convince ourselves rationally that by analogy we can expand our ideas mathematically and logically to cover the whole universe. We believe that the natural laws we observe on earth apply and operate in exactly the same way everywhere in the universe. We could hardly think otherwise. We have no other knowledge of nature except that which comes through our earthly observations. Even our modern astronomy is based mostly on earthbound observations.[5]

Nevertheless, the fundamental dilemma remains: how can our observations and analytical ideas and theories be trusted if modern naturalism is true? They are not independent of the process of cause and effect. Observations and theoretical interpretations are subject to false assumptions, poor logic, prejudice, misunderstanding, misperception, and carelessness, but the most serious concern, by far, is the problem of the mind's lacking independence from the chemical and physical processes it is supposedly studying.

The Loss of Freedom

When one goes to purchase an automobile or an encyclopedia, or for that matter almost anything, why do the salesmen always say that their company, or their product, is the best? Why do they not recommend alternatives? The answer is obvious. They have a vested interest. They are employed by their company to sell that particular product, and they are trained to think only of the good points of their product and the weak points of their competitors. The analogy is not perfect by any means, but the point may, nevertheless, be pressed. One who is controlled by a larger reality is not completely free to be objective about that reality. The more control there is, the less objectivity there will be. A truly nonbiased evaluation of a product must come from a source independent and free of control or influence by the companies involved.

The modern worldview allows no objectivity because it defines the mind simply as an effect of the process. The mind is thus controlled by the process. It is not free in the traditional sense of that term. *Freedom* is a term used by modern naturalists to describe mental activity that is too complex to be easily predicted, but the worldview of naturalism has no source of or basis for real freedom. On the other hand, God could freely choose to grant intellectual freedom to mankind because God is an absolutely free and sovereign being, but there is no basis for true freedom if nature is the only reality.

Physical indeterminacy at the subatomic level (the famous Heisenberg principle) is in no sense a source for true freedom. Currently indeterminacy and modern chaos theories describe, among other things, our inability to predict every movement of individual subatomic particles, but statistically the overall patterns of movement or change seem to be quite regular. Radioactive materials, for example, have a distinct half-life that may be calculated with some significant degree of precision, even though no one has been able to figure out a way to predict which atom in the material will disintegrate next. Such seemingly random yet ordered natural phenomena, however, are no basis at all for affirming responsible, intellectual freedom.

Freedom has been lost in the modern worldview. Ironically modern people seek freedom perhaps more intensely than any other generation of mankind, yet in their quest to free themselves from God, they have destroyed all hope of ever achieving true freedom. Such a consequence is the great surprise of modern thought.

The Loss of Truth

When Hegel, in the nineteenth century, outlined what he saw as the dialectical development of history and of thought, he concluded that the outcome would be absolute freedom. The true reality, he argued, was neither static, nor was it nothing. It was neither being nor nonbeing. Reality, according to Hegel, was in essence a synthesis of being and nonbeing. Thus *reality* was dynamically *becoming*. It was dialectically, rationally, unfolding and growing. Nothing was stable. As a result, there could be no absolute truth. There might be true statements at a given time, but truth as an absolute whole was always changing, developing, and growing. In other words, truth was relative to the moment, and thus it lost many of its essential attributes. Truth as a permanent, unchanging, correct relationship between thought and reality no longer existed. It could not exist because there no longer was a stable created reality that could be known, according to Hegel's modern worldview.

Dialectical progress was supposed to lead to freedom, but the loss of truth has most noticeably resulted in a loss of freedom in almost every area of life. This is the case politically. Where naturalism has come to dominate a society, there has been a loss of political freedom. Moral accountability is lost when freedom is lost, and all forms of naturalism and most forms of idealism ultimately fail in their efforts to justify a moral code.[6] More significant, however, has been the philosophical loss of intellectual freedom. This loss is felt in many ways, even though it has not yet been formally recognized by many in the scientific community.[7] This same loss has also affected modern theological studies.

The Impact of Modern Thought on Theology

If biblical doctrine evolved and developed strictly by natural principles—such as purely economic, political, cultural, and social forces—from the religious milieu of ancient Israel, then theological beliefs can ultimately be nothing more than cultural products and/or anomalies. Modern theological scholars often suggest that the people of Israel symbolized future hopes in mythological stories set in the past. So the early chapters of Genesis are considered by many to be carefully crafted theological revisions of standard ancient Near Eastern myths arising perhaps out of the eschatology of ancient Israel's messianic hope.[8] If Messiah is to bring peace and righteousness in the future, maybe he is actually restoring a lost paradise of the past. Therefore, according to many modern biblical critics, the Genesis account of Eden possibly originated during or soon after the Babylonian Exile when messianic hopes grew. Supposedly ideas of paradise were advanced ideas of Persian origin and thus probably were not a part of early, primitive Israelite thought.

This evolutionary theory of theological development is, however, based on the modern worldview that sees all of reality in this evolutionary pattern. What is not so easily seen is that such a pattern of development also makes the Bible primarily an antiquarian book, of interest to scholars who specialize in such things perhaps but having little if any modern relevance. We may allegorize or devotionalize or draw morals from the stories, as Aesop did from his fables, in an effort to establish societal norms, but there certainly is no room for divinely inspired propositional revelation within this modern theory of origins.

We may get helpful moral hints from the Bible. We may find the literature historically interesting. We may be fascinated by the history of religious ideas. We may even learn to appreciate the theology expressed by the ancient writers and consider it to be profound. Nevertheless, if these biblical ideas were culturally originated and strictly determined by evolutionary processes, then our interest in them is also culturally originated and determined, as are our conclusions about the various issues raised. Our feelings of interest and appreciation may be authentic, but our theology can only be strictly subjective and relative.

If our minds naturally evolved exclusively from biological processes, they can only function in certain predetermined ways. This predetermination, however, is not by a loving God who is free and able to grant us responsible intellectual freedom. Rather, this predetermination is by unthinking chemicals and blind chance. How can we trust such a source to provide that which is necessary for truth and freedom? The answer is that we cannot.

CHAPTER 4

MODERN THEISTIC ALTERNATIVES

NOT ALL MODERN THINKERS have accepted full-blown naturalism. Many continue to work philosophically and scientifically within the framework of modern advancement thought but nevertheless personally affirm some form of theism. This is not the biblical theism of the earlier worldview, but these thinkers recognize that naturalism cannot be true. These new theisms, however, are often adopted because they are seen as opening new doors for truth and freedom and because they have explanatory power and relevance.

One of the most promising of the modern theories is known as panentheism or process theology.[1] This new theism has grown out of the process philosophy of Alfred North Whitehead that in turn was developed to help interpret the startling new information coming to light from physical chemistry and from recent studies in nuclear physics.[2]

The New Physics

From ancient times the scientific quest has been a search for the basic substance out of which all things are made. If we knew what things were made of, perhaps we could control them or manipulate them, so the scientists thought. Recent discoveries have challenged those basic assumptions.

Nature, it seems, is not essentially made out of a substance of any sort. Matter itself is only an illusion of substantiality. This illusion is a reality produced by chemical bonding. This bonding between atoms is a mysterious force made up of minute interlocking electro-magnetic potentialities, positive and negative charges. An even more mysterious aspect of reality is the composition of the atom itself.

Neat models made from Ping-Pong balls and sticks illustrate many features of chemical or atomic structures, but the models are not literal. Electrons are not small planets in orbit around a central sun, though that model continues to serve as a helpful tool for explaining some aspects of macroreality. Apparently the atom is actually made up of an array of electromagnetic vibrations. A maze of positive electrostatic charges are organized, along with a series of "safe particles" that seem either to have no permanent charge or else exist in a neutral state, into a group called the nucleus, which is sur-rounded in most cases by multiple shells of negatively charged energy.

This tiny package of energy is characterized by incessant activity and change within inherent limits. These limits are definite, how-ever, and they enable scientists to classify and define the elements. Yet the electrons and the protons of the phosphorous atom are in themselves seemingly no different from the electrons and protons of the sodium atom or any other atom. The quantity of energy is unique to each atomic unit, and the structural characteristics vary, but the underlying reality of all things seems to be the same. That which is the same may be thought of as spinning waves of energy. This "energy in motion" is the common basis of all existence as we know it today, according to currently accepted scientific theory.[3]

Time is a functional measurement of this process, and space is a quantitative measurement. Perpetual motion, which at our common human level of perception is impossible, seems to be the norm of basic reality. Everything hums!

How then can one account for this living state of all things? Does motion need a source? Is there an organizing principle that creates the structures of elemental reality? If so, is this principle intelligent?

Could a nonintelligent principle structure reality in such a way as to produce human intelligence? This is no trivial question. The absence of God in scientific textbooks may well be the most fundamental error of all.

Modern Process Theology

The most fundamental level of reality from the modern scientific viewpoint is the underlying subatomic process of existence. Some thinkers claim to have recognized a similarity between this fundamental activity that pervades the universe and the logically necessary descriptive characteristics of God. To be the supreme reality, God would logically have to be the source of the fundamental structures of reality. Modern scientific research has concluded that the subatomic process creates the structures of reality. Traditionally God is described as supremely powerful, yet scientifically speaking the subatomic process contains the totality of potential power in the physical universe. God is mysteriously omnipresent, as is the process. God determines the future, as does the process.

Assume for the moment that this theory of an underlying process of interactive energy is true. It is not at all hard to consider, in a philosophical sense, the likely nature of this fundamental process. First, the process would be the ultimately necessary reality upon which all other levels of reality depend. Second, the process would include all of nature but perhaps could be more than nature since it would contain within itself the sum total of all potentiality, the future itself. Third, events that happen could become fixed in memory—that is, continuing patterns could be established and, in some sense, preserved within the process. History would not exist in the same way that the present exists, but every event of every present moment would leave its imprint on the process and thus have an effect on the next moment.

The future is made up of the seemingly infinite potential of possible events, but the past, shaped by all previous events, would influence the present in the "selection" process whereby some of these future possibilities become actualities. Some potentials occur—that is, they are actualized—and thus they become present realities and then instantly are fixed as historical actualities. Other potential events are rejected or avoided and thus never occur. This then is a technical description of existence, the moment-by-moment reality experienced by the fundamental level of interactive energy.

According to modern process philosophy, the human mind would be a level of reality produced by the process, in keeping with theories of biological evolution, but the mind is so sophisticated that it has actually begun to mirror the process in some ways. The mind is in some sense an image of the process; it functions in the likeness of the process in that the mind has become aware of history and the future. Human choice is a gift of the process, which by nature is an actualizer of potentials. Nevertheless, if this model were true, mankind remains in no sense separate from nature, but nature would not be properly thought of as impersonal. (See figure 4.)

In order to know the process, man must study nature, including himself—in particular, his own mind. Those who affirm this process to be a theistic reality claim that this opens new doors to both truth and freedom. We can know the truth, they say, because the actualized reality of history is fixed. We may not know the truth, for we may be mistaken about many things, but fixed reality can be examined from within the present.

Since the present is in a real sense determined by the past—that is to say, since the actual conditions of the present occur as a result of the mix between the options available and the patterns established previously—one may start from the present, which is, of course, the only place we can start from, and examine it. Through tracing out the surviving evidence in the processional present, we support our concepts of the past. Generally, this surviving evidence will be artifacts that continue to exist in the present from the past or currently existing documents of primary or secondary sources of information

Figure 4

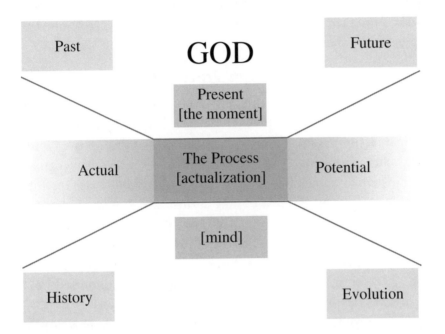

about the past. Where clear evidence does not survive, we must make cautious judgments; for the reality of the historical past is enormously complex, but the doorway to historical truth is at least open, claim the process thinkers.

Similarly, scientific truth can be known, for the process is orderly, regular, and consistent, at least statistically. By carefully observing the present and by rational deduction and analogy, we can know the past. By knowing the past and observing the present, we can scientifically predict some aspects of the future. For example, by careful observation scientists can and have discovered patterns that have been established in the process and that seem likely to continue: the so-called natural laws.

Despite the real existence of those patterns or laws, process theologians nevertheless maintain a doctrine of freedom. The future is always open, they say, because the possibilities are infinite. The immediate future is not as open as the distant future, but the possibilities for novelty, choice, and freshness are always there. Freedom is future oriented. The process works through the available options, influenced by the past, yet truly open to the future.[4]

The Problems of Process Thought

Does this theistic processism solve the epistemological problems raised by the modern worldview? There are, no doubt, many positive features of process thinking. It is clearly an advance over traditional naturalism. It is based on an improved science. It recognizes the Einsteinian revolution in physics, and it builds on carefully researched data. Newtonian physics seemed absolute in its day, and yet it was in some ways wrong. Thus, one hesitates to rule out even more radically new intellectual revolutions in the future as the intense research continues, but clearly the new process philosophy is seeking truth and freedom, and it is attempting to build itself upon the actual scientific data of experience.

Several problems emerge, however, when we carefully reflect on this new theistic theory. Perhaps the most obvious one is why it should be called theism. How could one know that the process is God? If the question is purely semantic, then process theology may simply be mystical science. A major difficulty with all attempts to build theism out of the modern worldview is the inherent ambiguity of the evidence; but there are other specific epistemological difficulties with this particular form of theism, and they are of a rather serious nature.

First, mankind is necessarily a part of the process. We look at the process from within. We are not, then, objective observers at all. Our thoughts must be formed by our past, just as the overall process of reality is shaped by its past. An individual may have a new thought, but it will come only from the range of available options. We may believe, as process philosophy claims, that the options are potentially infinite, but how can that be anything other than a wishful speculation? No one can know the status of potentially available options if he or she can stand only in the present and peer into the future through the glasses of the fixed actualities of the past.

If man is wholly a product of the natural process, at what point does he transcend the process? If he does not transcend it, and if he has no transcendent source of information, then his knowledge can never be objectively justified.

Significantly, no one can know that the process transcends nature either. We want to argue that the process is more than nature, but we have no necessary or sufficient grounds on which to do so. Unless we have already adopted a monistic view of reality, the mere existence of the process does not require that the process contains the potential future. The existence of the process may imply an ability to actualize potentials, but to suggest that this ability is an attribute of a natural process that is self-existent, self-explanatory, and self-sustaining is to speculate with a naturalistic bias.

It is gratuitous to speak of the process as selecting from among the options. It is anthropomorphic to describe the process as if it were a mind remembering the past and considering the future. What data requires the process to differ from blind randomness, pure chance, or simple chemical and physical interaction? Thus figure 4 becomes figure 3, and the old dilemmas of traditional naturalism reappear.

Why Modern Thought Fails

Suppose someone were to argue that the process had to transcend nature as it exists in the present or else evolution could not have occurred. Perhaps they would claim that there must be unrealized potential since novelty has from time to time appeared, as demonstrated by the fossil record, for example. Or the argument might be that the process is itself transcended by the bipolar reality of the actualized past and the potential future. It is not the process as such that is God, they might say, but the totality of actual and potential reality. Potentiality then becomes the philosophical basis for explaining how evolution could happen. The actualized past preserved by fossils that exist in the present would then be used to explain how evolution did happen.

Since one product of this evolutionary process is a personal being, the totality of reality must include personal traits and characteristics. Before man evolved, those personal characteristics were strictly potential, and thus they would have transcended the actualized reality. The dynamic process supposedly brought these characteristics into a state of actualization. Evolution occurred. The point, however, is that this theory must go on to contend that there is still infinite potential within the transcendent part of the "God/process." Personality, as humans experience it now, may one day be viewed as being as primitive as the consciousness of a beetle appears to us today.

This concept of transcendence, however, has a deadly hook in it. Almost by definition, the future will invalidate even our most sophisticated theories of the present. Truth has again become relative to the moment. We may have some truth about the actualized past since it is now fixed, but even this is by no means assured. In the future we may discover that there is a subprocess reality that is of a different order from anything previously considered. Such a subprocess reality would make the process that we know about only an effect, not a source.[5] This would revolutionize our science, and it could easily invalidate today's best philosophical theories.

Truth, as it has been traditionally defined, does not exist necessarily in this modern scientific worldview. There are only momentary correctness, warranted assertions, and majority opinions. Therefore, the theistic alternative of process thought turns out to be capable of being believed only at the moment. It could not claim eternal significance for any spiritual victory in the past, such as the cross of Christ. It cannot even be sure that real mental, moral freedom exists. The subprocess reality may be coldly deterministic, or it may be random. In either case responsible freedom is once again an illusion.

Can we trust our minds to give us the truth about reality if our minds are only a product of that reality, even if they are a product achieved from a transcendent array of potential options? The answer is no.

We may find that our ideas are useful and that they enable us to accomplish fantastic feats. We can put men into space, take close-up pictures of the rings of Saturn, watch comets crash into Jupiter, or listen to electromagnetic discharges from distant stars. We can build washing machines, automobiles, television systems, and computers. Our thoughts are definitely useful, but we have no assurance that they are either true or free in any responsible sense. The relativism of modern thought is no less self-defeating than is the relativism of many earlier non-theistic, nonbiblical philosophies.

Modern theories first lost their significance philosophically. Eventually, this philosophical weakness will filter down to the public who will again become disillusioned and frustrated by the meaninglessness of pure technology and by the randomness and purposelessness of their lives. So they will seek significance in human sexual relationships or in mysticism or religious ritual. The patterns of this seeking have all been seen before, and they always seem to result in greater alienation, loss of hope, and widespread depression and despair. Such a scenario does not demonstrate progress and advancement. It might well be a sign of spiritual warfare.

Open Theism

Another theistic alternative that seeks to preserve freedom within the modern mind-set is known as open theism.[6] Like process theism, the openness view considers the future to be a set of possibilities. The theory challenges traditional theism's view that God foreknows the future. The future, they say, is not fixed, and thus God cannot know it infallibly. God knows it as a set of possibilities, but supposedly he does not know which possibilities will become actual. Thus, God is in some ways like the process of process theism. He is unlike the process in that he is a conscious being who can cause certain things to happen if he has committed himself to them; thus, biblical predictive prophecy is legitimate, but in all things not specifically determined by God's power, the future is open. God knows all that can be known, but the future cannot be known, for it is a set of open options.

This view, like process theism, is attempting to solve some traditional theological problems—the problem of evil, for example: God simply does not know ahead of time what is going to happen, and thus he cannot be blamed for all the evil that has happened. Open theism is also attempting to incorporate modern scientific understandings of cosmology and physics.

The view claims that Scripture supports the idea that God does not know all things and often changes his mind when confronted with unexpected circumstances. Traditional views of omniscience are said to be based on Greek notions of divine attributes and infinity rather than on biblical notions of a dynamic, "changing" God.

Can Open Theism Be True?

Traditional theists should be willing to review the biblical evidence, but it is not as if the open theists have discovered new texts previously unknown to Reformed or Catholic theologians. Exegetical guidelines—context, canonical harmony, theological consistency, along with grammatical regularities and syntactical options—may be followed in support of both viewpoints. But is the future truly open? Is our lack of knowledge about the future due to its complexity or its indeterminancy? Is God causing the flow of history, or is it a free and autonomous reality? Does the future already exist in a variety of time lines, as *Star Trek* fiction would suggest, or does it come into being out of nothing?

Open theism has offered its alternative in a day when traditional views are being challenged on every hand. The answers it gives, however, fail at a basic level. How can one find meaning in a world where even God does not always know what is true or right or best? Where can one's mind rest if even God's claims and affirmations may not be settled truths?

Open theists often are evangelical Christians who trust the Bible and even affirm its inerrancy and infallibility. To be fair, they need not, and do not, argue that everything is open. God may well have settled some things but not all things. In their view this leaves room for freedom and for greater human responsibility. Unfortunately, open theism accomplishes this by taking a position in some ways similar to the garden serpent of Genesis 3. The serpent said God was wrong in the sense that he lied. God said, "Eat of the tree of the knowledge of good and evil, and you will die," but the serpent claimed that God had other motives and thus spoke a known untruth. To accept the serpent's perspective was the original temptation that led to original sin.

Open theists do not put it quite that way. According to them, God does not speak a known untruth, he is no liar, but God does speak some things that he might be wrong about. He does not know the future infallibly because he cannot know the free acts of moral agents. He can say what he will do "if," but he could not know which *if* will occur since the choices are real. Regardless of various biblical examples that might seem to imply this lack of divine knowledge, the simplest way to conceptualize this kind of scenario seems to be on the scientific model of nature described above. The present is real and in process; the past is fixed in divine memory; the future is open because it is simply a set of undetermined potentials as described above.

Theists, however, lose more than they gain under this openness model. God created the universe that exists. He designed the system to accomplish his purpose. To suggest that God would not know what would happen in his creation is a difficult concept to grasp. If nature were fundamentally random, then it could not be known with certainty, but that raises all the problems of how randomness achieves intelligence through random natural processes. A created world is not random, however, so why would it be essentially unknown or unknowable by its Creator? If there is an intelligent design that has been implemented by a creator, it is difficult to conceive how this could produce a truly open result.[7]

Discussions of open theism are fascinating intellectual exercises for theologians, and the view is not likely to go away. The openness view, however, has been unable to develop a consistent worldview. A Creator God must at least know what he is creating, and given what we know about the universe, it demonstrates a structure that transcends the subatomic indeterminacy. The universe is not random, and it is not self-explanatory. The universe is held together and sustained moment by moment by intelligent design. This purposive power is not found in matter itself. God is the One providing the order and the process, and it is thus contradictory to propose that God does not know the future, even the future actions of free moral agents. It is much easier to explain how God can sovereignly choose to maintain uncoercive knowledge of a free moral action than it is to explain the intentional creation of an unknowable and/or unpredictable process, mystifying even to its Designer.

If open theism were true, how could one know that it was true? One could not know that God does not know the future. The Bible never tells us things that God does not know. That God allows suffering does not prove that he did not know it would come. That God redeems from sin rather than preventing sin does not prove that God was unaware of the future when Adam was formed. The supposed benefits of an open future are offset by the loss of assurance that God is sufficient. Without a fixed reference point in God's knowledge, there is no final basis for meaning. Ultimately, God is naturalized, and the modern worldview prevails.

CHAPTER 5

WHAT IS
NATURALISTIC EVOLUTION?

EVOLUTION IS A PHILOSOPHICAL MODEL by which the world may be interpreted in terms of *change* rather than *stability*. Biological facts, for example, can be and in modern times have been organized by this model (i.e., organic evolution). Evolution, however, is an interpretive system based on process and change that has effectively encompassed the scientific mind even beyond the realm of biology. Naturalism is the dominant worldview that guides modern scientific thinking and controls scientific methodology, and thus naturalistic evolution has come to be considered by many as if it were a general law rather than simply a scientific theory (i.e., an interpretive model). Evolution itself had an almost unchallengeable status in late twentieth-century science and philosophy. Will it hold this status throughout the twenty-first century as well? Or will some other model supplant it?

Seven Assumptions of Evolutionary Biology

A philosophical model that serves as a basic and comprehensive interpretive framework for scientific study should be able to be stated clearly and spelled out in some detail. Thus, the assumptions of evolutionary theories should be definable. There are at least seven of these basic intellectual elements that together outline the essential structure of the naturalistic version of the biological theory of evolution.[1]

First, it is assumed that *physical similarity among living beings is an indication of a historical biological linkage.* In other words, if there is a significant structural similarity between two or more species, this supposedly indicates that there is a relatively close relationship historically and biologically between the organisms possessing that similarity.[2] Thus, for example, it is assumed that all vertebrates are genetically related to one another in a historical and developmental sense, as well as in the physical sense of having a backbone as a central element of the skeletal structure. This means that all living things with a backbone are thought to have had a common ancestor, whatever the first creature was to have had a backbone. No one assumes the backbone evolved more than once in the same way with the same result in two or more species. Backbones are complex structures. It would also be assumed that all creatures with gills are genetically related to one another and have a common ancestor, and all mammals are genetically related to one another because gills and wombs, like backbones, are much too complex to have naturalistically and by chance originated more than once.

Second, the assumption is made that at an earlier stage of evolutionary development *modern vertebrates and invertebrates had a series of common ancestors.* This is in keeping with the even more general assumption (to be elaborated as number four below) that supposes all life on earth to be related genetically and to have developed from prior life forms that had not yet manifested these genetic differentiations. The demand of the evolutionary theory for the unity of all living things is strong enough to go beyond the demand of the first assumption, stated above, for physical similarity in obvious ways, such as backbones or internal gestation and live birth. Naturalistic evolution looks for and must find even more basic similarities, such as the particular carbon-based molecules that constitute living matter. When this common foundation for life is found, the naturalistic mind concludes that naturalism has been proven true. The problem is, such evidence is equally supportive of theories of intelligent design. A wise designer could build all life according to a pattern that could include a common organic chemistry.

Third, it is assumed (without any experimental data) that *metazoan life spontaneously arose from the protozoans*. Even protozoan (single cell) creatures are extremely complex.[3] No one would suggest even a remote likelihood that multicellular living creatures could have spontaneously originated from nonliving matter.

Fourth, the fundamental assumption from which the first three grow is that *all life on earth is genetically related and thus arose from a common ancestor*, that is, a single cell. Everything from the virus to the whale supposedly has developed from common ancestors. Some of these ancestors are now extinct, and some are purely hypothetical, since there is no fossil evidence of their existence. The fossils that do exist lead some scientists to conclude (or we might say, to speculate) that other living forms also existed that are not preserved as fossils. In fact, it is generally thought that many creatures that did exist at one time did not have a single specimen preserved in the fossil record. This is a critical component of this philosophical model because the argument is that these many other living forms would, if they ever were to be found in the fossil record, fill in the gaps in the physical evidence currently available. This presently unavailable evidence supposedly would show that a continuous succession of living forms did arise from one another gradually through the years. There are, of course, huge gaps in the chain of evidence we actually have. There are virtually no indisputable transitional forms[4] in the fossil record between any of the taxonomic groups, and there is most certainly no physical evidence of any kind that transitional organisms have ever existed between the major classifications, such as between vertebrates and invertebrates.[5] That all living forms, in clearly describable ways, are genetically related to one another remains, however, a necessary assumption of modern evolutionary biology. Intelligent design theory may equally find similarity to be a reasonable expectation of the design model, but it would not conclude that physical similarity proves biological descent.

Fifth, *nonliving matter spontaneously gave rise to living matter.* This is the most basic assumption of all modern materialistic and naturalistic philosophy. It is often argued that this is the only possible "scientific" position. On this naturalistic assumption, so the argument goes, scientific research into the question of biological origins can continue indefinitely without dogmatic theological limitations, and the various supposed processes by which life could have arisen may be studied. Supposedly, a creationist has no motivation to study creative processes since one could not study an exclusively divine process using traditional scientific methods. Perhaps the correct process, as naturalistic science might propose, could be duplicated in a laboratory, and a new virus or another living cell might be generated from nonliving chemicals.[6] This continuing research may tell us the nature of the forces that affected the earliest development of life and thus may enable us to understand the factors that influenced this development. Such knowledge would perhaps prove relevant to biological science in general and could even provide useful information about the true nature of life itself, about the feasibility of finding life elsewhere in the universe, or even about the future possibilities for controlling or influencing human evolution. On the other hand, the naturalistic argument continues; to say that biogenesis was a supernatural act of God is to remove the cause, the process, and the event from natural causality altogether. It would, therefore, be a nonscientific (i.e., a nonnaturalistic) conclusion. There would be no scientific cause or process to discover, because science, by the naturalistic definition, must deal only with naturalistic facts. Therefore, no scientific observation or experiment could discover a supernatural cause or process or event.[7]

Sixth, *spontaneous biogenesis occurred only once,* or, what for all practical purposes amounts to the same thing, *the whole of present-day biological life has arisen from a single primeval cell.* This assumption is not strictly necessary, but it is almost always assumed. At this stage of our scientific knowledge, the alternative—a multiple origin of living cells—is considered to be impossible. The reason for this assumption is simple. The genetic code for all forms of life has the same structure. This genetic code makes up the DNA and the RNA molecules that spell out, as it were, all of the instructions needed for chemically making each different part of each different living thing. For identical genetic coding systems to have spontaneously and independently arisen from a random process that occurred by chance is simply unacceptable because it is incredibly improbable.[8] That the genetic code arose even once would not be believable on statistical grounds, for it can be shown to be a highly improbable event,[9] but it is necessary to believe that it happened once since it is presently in existence. It is not necessary to believe that this complex event happened twice in exactly the same way, and virtually no one does believe this. Intelligent design, on the other hand, is not necessarily limited to a single physical point of origin.

Seventh, *the process by which all* multicelled *life forms developed from one another* and originally from single-celled life forms *was one of spontaneous random mutation and natural selection.* Perhaps a stray cosmic ray struck the nucleus of a reproducing cell, or perhaps in some other as yet unexplained way, a variation was introduced into the genetic code of a reproducing cell, altering its encoded pattern of information. This variation would change the offspring. Perhaps in some rare case the change would allow the new cell or cells to adapt better, adjust better to a changing environment, or develop features that would enable it to survive in a different or perhaps in a more efficient way. Such changes might, then, be preserved by the natural fact that this changed cellular structure conceivably could make that living form more secure and safe. This newly organized cell or pattern of cells may be more appropriately adapted to its environment, or the organism may be more efficient in food gathering or energy usage. Those mutations—by far the vast majority—that weaken the offspring or leave it less adapted to its environment would not generally be preserved due to the simple fact that the strong tend to survive and the weak perish.[10]

Those mutations that led to some life forms being excessively prolific, for example, might tend to increase the survival chances of that form of life. Mutations that decreased reproduction rates, or the simple lack of helpful mutations despite a changing environment, or mutations that physically weakened the offspring would tend to cause that life form to become extinct or at least to decrease in numbers. It is, of course, assumed by the theory of evolution that the overall thrust of this process is to develop toward increased adaptability. This is what has supposedly produced the multivaried life forms now present on the earth, according to naturalistic evolutionary theory.

The facts, however, show that sometimes the strong are hurt or killed (by fighting or by accident, perhaps), and sometimes the weak survive and reproduce prolifically. Thus, the odds against the natural success of evolutionary theory increase. Nevertheless, evolutionists tend to fall back on their most characteristic reply when faced with the statistical evidence against their view: however improbable, evolution did in fact succeed, because as can plainly be seen, multivaried life forms do currently exist on the earth. Somehow the assumption of evolution has become the proof of evolution, and the obvious fallacy of such reasoning is ignored.

Mankind is thought to be the most important advance of the natural, environmental process. Mankind stands at the head of the evolutionary class. As incredible as it may seem, evolution supposedly has now come to understand itself as mankind has achieved twentieth-century scientific knowledge. Most evolutionists also believe that the fossils document the history of this evolutionary development, and in its standard form, the theory explains the factual data without recourse to supernatural causes or activities.

These seven assumptions together establish the framework of the modern evolutionary model for interpreting biological data. These are clearly elements of a philosophical theory, for none of these seven axioms can be proven experimentally. Even if one or another of them could be experimentally shown to be possible (for example, perhaps by using some kind of radiation, someone might one day induce a mutation in a protozoa that observably results in a metazoan life form), this would by no means prove that such an event actually occurred in the historical development of life. At best, such evidence would only show that the third assumption was not totally unrealistic; it could have happened. The evidence does not currently support this possibility, however, and it is not at all certain that we are empirically justified in claiming that this step is anything more than just barely conceivable.

To demonstrate genetic similarity is not to prove physical descent or even physical relationship. To argue that similarity proves descent or relationship is clearly an example of circumstantial reasoning, for a common design employed by a singular creative force, to enable different life forms to survive in a common environment, would produce the same effect. If we were to see five different paintings with similar characteristics in a museum, we would not conclude that the paintings descended from one another. Rather, we would suppose the existence of a common artist, or at least we would understand how a common style and technique could be used by several artists with common interests and perspectives. Similarities in living matter could also result from a common design by one or more creators.[11]

Thus, the seven assumptions summarized above do not arise from strictly experimental science. They are elements of a worldview. They can be modified by individual thinkers, though the modifications cannot be substantial ones if naturalism is to be maintained. These seven elements in some form seem to be necessary if the theory of naturalistic biological evolution is to stand at all. If any one of them were to be denied, the others would in turn lose their force as well.[12] The naturalistic worldview of the advancement is an interrelating system of ideas, each depending on the others.

Ten Axioms of Modern Scientific Thought

So persuasive has this naturalistic philosophical model of biological evolution become that it seems to be no longer open for discussion within the scientific establishment.[13] The most interesting development in twentieth-century science, however, was the fact that the *evolutionary model grew beyond biology.* Evolution is no longer strictly a biological theory. It has *become an interpretative model for virtually all modern scientific thinking.*[14] Astronomers discuss the *evolution* of the universe. Sociologists discuss the *evolution* of society. And so through all the various fields of study, the basic principles of evolutionary theory are extended.[15] This has led to a much broader understanding of the theory. The seven assumptions named above outline the implications of this interpretative philosophical model for biological studies. As a worldview, however, naturalism speaks to issues beyond those of biological science. These ten broader assumptions or axioms seem to define modern naturalistic scientific thinking in general.

First, *something is eternal.* This is affirmed because it is correctly assumed that something real exists now. There simply is no evidence at all that would lead one to assume that something real arises from absolutely nothing. Someone could claim that it may happen, but by the nature of the case, such a thing could not be understood or evidentially confirmed. There would be no explanation, no reason, no cause, if that from which something arose were known to be absolutely nothing. It would not be that the cause was simply unknown, as if with further study it might become known—for if it is really nothing, then there is not an "it" to discover and eventually know.[16] It would be utterly absurd and innately contradictory and thus self-destructive to attempt to affirm intelligently that something arose from true and complete nothing. Therefore, an axiom of all intelligent thinking is that something is eternal.

Second, *physical matter/energy is the eternal something*. This is difficult to express properly in a single sentence, for the terms *physical matter/energy* could be misleading. Whatever it is that constitutes the various subatomic particles is what is meant. That form of energy out of which electrons and protons are made, that condition or state which is capable of expressing polarity, that existing reality that has potential—this is what is thought to be eternal. Out of this reality the atomic structures formed.[17] Out of those elements the molecules and the substance of the universe were formed.

Third, *physical matter/energy relationships give rise to physical matter/energy processes*. Relationships include proximity. If the fundamental reality were to produce a negative charge and a positive charge in close proximity to each other, these charges would interact to produce several processes including perhaps relative motion. To state this axiom is not to say that modern science fully understands exactly how these relationships would occur, but it is assumed that real relationships did occur within a previously eventless matrix and that processes of various kinds naturally resulted.[18]

Fourth, *physical matter/energy processes are inherently structural*. For example, opposite polarities attract and like polarities repel. This clearly rules out some "logically possible" combinations of physical matter/energy. We do not have a stable atom with electrons only and no protons. Logically, we could have three electrons clinging together, but actually we would not have such a combination. It would be unstable, and even if for a moment such a structure were to appear, it would not remain a viable part of reality. The nature of physical matter/energy is such that it has certain inherent structural possibilities and certain impossibilities. Those possibilities that actually occur and are stable would perhaps tend to exist in more abundance.

Fifth, *physical matter/energy processes inherently tend toward stability.* Unstable structures tend to disintegrate and break apart. They do not last even if by chance they should form. The dynamic nature of the physical matter/energy processes assures this result.

Sixth, *physical matter/energy processes are random.* They may tend toward stability, but they are not rigid. They do not always move immediately to the most stable condition. Potentially, they can occur in unexpected forms at any time. By nature they are statistically regular, but in specific cases they seem to be indeterminate.

Seventh, *the interaction of physical matter/energy processes tends to produce potential.* This interaction may simply be relative motion, or it might be a chemical reaction when two entities come into contact. In any case, the assumption is that somehow potential is produced where previously there was none. Intelligent design theory, not naturalism, argues that the rise of potential does not come from the absence of potential but requires a highly organized source. Naturalistic thought, however, simply postulates the rise of potential from mere interaction.

Eighth, *potential produces the possibility of stabilizations at higher orders of complexity.* This is the possibility that fortunately occurred, but there is no necessity in this process. Naturalists believe that at least in this one case this most fortunate result came to be, and thus we are here.

Ninth, *higher orders of complexity may occur in localized situations due to energy interactions within the overall stabilizing process.*

The fifth axiom is the most dominant one. It is the reasonable basis for the second law of thermodynamics, and thus it seems to be confirmed by all known processes, but axiom six is the key for naturalistic philosophy. Axiom seven is clearly testable. The laws of thermodynamics based on axiom five predict that axiom seven simply will never occur, but chance (axiom six) is the necessary, though unpredictable, factor in naturalistic philosophy. The overall tendency is to stabilize, but if chance governs the processes—within the inherent structural limits, of course—then it might conceivably produce in some localized areas a potential for increased orders of complexity. Evolutionists contend that these more complex structures may also be stable and thus may survive and adapt to their environment.

Theists have contended that bare potential is an insufficient basis upon which to account for the actualization of anything, much less a higher order of complexity. Some actual cause is necessary to bring about an actual result, and an increase in complexity at least requires a template or a preexisting pattern. A situation that is purely potential has no causal trigger. Even if some hypothetical reality could be conceived according to this model, the actual reality we have cannot be thus conceived. The present universal contingency would not arise spontaneously, because every actualized reality that we can observe has an actual cause. The issue is the natural state of the reality that we must account for, the universe as it is now.

This universe gives every evidence of being caused and arranged by an intelligent mind, and yet it demonstrates no likelihood of being self-caused, which appears to be both a logical and a factual impossibility in any case, or self-arranged and organized.[19] Such arguments have been ignored for the most part by advancement thinkers, however, because those arguments imply that an actual cause other than the universe itself—in whole or in part—would have to exist in order for physical reality to exist in the form that it now exists, and advancement thought has steadfastly set itself against such views. Reality must have an exclusively natural explanation, they say, but it doesn't require a cause that is fundamentally unlike all other caused reality. Nevertheless, modern naturalists continue to maintain their naturalism even at the risk of denying all hope for any rational justification of their view. Reason itself is at stake.

Tenth, *the earth is a local situation in which the potential for increasing complexity has overcome the general tendency toward stabilization or decay.* In other words, on the earth, due to a random chance collection of positive factors—available energy[20] and suitable environment, both occurring early enough and lasting long enough—life has evolved. This is thought by some modern evolutionists to be an almost inevitable occurrence on any planet or moon where the factors are available that make for a suitable local situation, but even if that proves not to be so, they still believe it happened in this one case.

These ten axioms of modern scientific thinking are then followed by the seven assumptions of evolutionary biology. Other scientific disciplines would build evolutionary assumptions relevant to their data upon these ten axioms as well. This is what modern naturalistic science understands reality to be.

CHAPTER 6

WHY NOT NATURALISTIC EVOLUTION?

THE RISE OF A NATURALISTIC CULTURAL CONSENSUS out of a previously theistic culture is surely a great surprise to some, but Bible believers are not surprised. The Scriptures warn over and over that the way leading to destruction is the broad way, the way more will travel. In the last days scoffers will come, denying that Christ came in the flesh, denying that God created all things, denying that salvation is by grace through faith in Christ alone.

What is new in our day is the denial of creation by scholars from within the church. The scientific method is far from infallible, as any review of intellectual history will show. On the other hand, the scientific method cannot be ignored as a source of much that is good in modern life. Naturalism, however, is false, and the evidence is compelling that this is so.

The Four Basic Beliefs of Modern Thinkers

Over the last half of the twentieth century, the following concepts came to govern the thinking of many Western people whether they were scientifically minded people or not. Public school textbooks, television programs, popular media, and the university setting reinforce these views even if they do not use these exact words. Unless one has religious commitments that challenge these views, the following ideas are generally affirmed:

First, *mankind evolved from animals.*

Second, *the human mind and human behavior are therefore directly influenced by our animal ancestry.*

Third, *all of reality is subject to naturalistic scientific investigation.*

Fourth, *truth is discoverable or at least confirmable by and only by the naturalistic scientific method of research.*[1]

These four dominant ideas of modern thinking have, of course, many essential corollaries. The first basic belief includes genetic mutations and natural selection (survival of the fittest) as essential procedural assumptions, for example; but in general, these four basic beliefs express the givens of modern secular Western thinking in the twentieth century.

In an even broader sense, all things are thought to be evolving. The actual process is from simple to complex to simple: from conception through birth to adulthood, then through old age to death. Supposedly, stars are born, and they go through various states, and then they die. Plant life has its cycle, and animal life does the same. By analogy the universe itself supposedly came into its present form through various stages, initiated by the so-called big bang explosion, and the overwhelming evidence is that it will one day experience a marked decline in available energy, and the whole universe will die and become still again.

This is the reality that, according to modern naturalistic advancement thought, is subject to scientific investigation, and this is the truth supposedly discovered by the modern scientific method of research. It is not an optimistic picture. Humans are explained by reference to lower forms of life. Modern humanity with all its advanced technology is only a brief stage in the overall process. The natural universe will itself inevitably decline and die. Mankind has no cosmic significance except perhaps as an entry in the metaphorical Cosmic Book of Records.[2]

Why then do people not lose hope and live in despair? Of course, some do! Some rebel against all established authority out of a sense of frustration. Meaninglessness is frightening. Fear and despair often go together.

Others remain optimistic by allowing feelings to substitute for reason. Some assume that people must make their own meaning by limiting their thinking to the pleasures of material gain or sensuality. The drug culture has found that certain chemicals bring desirable results when ingested, and since there is no enforceable moral norm in the natural universe, according to the modern worldview, the use of those chemicals is strictly, in this intellectual context, a personal decision. It's fun, so why not do it? Failing to find lasting pleasure in these temporal areas, naturalistic philosophy suggests that many will react by condemning temporal pleasure as sin and then seeking eternal pleasure either through achieving nonexistence (as in Eastern religions) or through achieving an imperishable, nonphysical, non-scientific, spiritual heaven (as in some modern forms of Western religions) that supposedly will not perish. In other words, religion, for the naturalistic philosopher, is simply grasping for straws. It is a manufactured meaning in a meaningless universe. It is an ancient alternative to truth. It is a set of mythologies that must now be replaced by the naturalistic reality modern science has discovered.

Even those who adopt a religious point of view, however, for the most part continue to believe that at the rational, physical level, evolution is the law of reality. This principle so dominates the rationality of modern thinkers that one cannot understand them without recognizing this fact. People, particularly in the West, often consider science to be the great oracle of truth, and science says that mankind has evolved from animal life, which in turn evolved from nonliving matter, which in turn came from an initial big bang. This is the reality in which twentieth-century Western thinkers live. Popular culture has accepted this framework also, and there is virtually no refuge from this powerful message.

Five Simple Objections to Naturalistic Evolution

Several objections to this naturalistic, evolutionary worldview of the advancement have been raised, though it cannot be said that these objections have changed many minds either within or without the scientific community.[3]

The second law of thermodynamics seems to be directly violated by evolutionary theory. The raw energy from the sun simply cannot direct the evolutionary process without a complex energy-conversion system, but that is exactly what must evolve according to naturalistic conceptions. The fossil record contains crucial gaps that are not obviously predictable according to evolutionary theory. Punctuated equilibrium is an after-the-fact explanation with little predictive power. Human minds are a qualitative jump, not just a quantitative one, above the animals.[4] There is no adequate, natural conversion system able to take random energy from the sun, or from any other natural source, and direct it into the production of order, thus causing the evolution of life out of nonliving matter. Moreover, the specific evidences and claims of evolutionary theory can often be (and have often been) challenged as well.[5]

These scientific arguments, and others like them, are often ineffective in academic debate, however, even though they are substantial arguments.[6] The reason for this ineffectiveness is that the issue is not simply one of factual science and evidence.[7] The issue is ultimately philosophical. It is one of worldview.[8] The range of physical similarities that so often are recited as compelling evidence for organic evolution can with equal facility stand as evidence for a common design. In fact, a simple case[9] can be made that suggests a fundamental weakness in naturalistic theories:

First, *materialism is not self-evidently true; in fact it likely is false.*[10] *In any case, scientific research does not depend upon naturalistic philosophy.* There is no factual evidence that requires naturalism. On the other hand, many phenomena and many systems are equally or at least arguably more successfully explained in terms of intelligent design. While some may argue that theism is not self-evident either, the existence of the genetic code implies a necessary source of information that is not found in the chemistry alone. In fact, life itself is unaccounted for by chemical organization alone. Rather, it seems that life rides on organized chemicals but is not produced merely by chemical complexity.[11]

Second, aside from all talk of natural selection, which has to occur outside of a controlled environment if evolution is true, even *artificial selection in a controlled environment has not been proven capable of producing an absolutely new kind of life-form.*[12] Even if polyploidy research or hybridization techniques do succeed in something similar to the production of a new species, the complexity and sophistication of the intelligently designed process involved in this production would argue against the chance reproduction of this process in nature. In evolutionary theory this event of new-species production must have happened over and over in nature literally thousands and millions of times. It is more than just a clever turn of the phrase to say that something must be there in order to be naturally selected. Natural selection is a conserving, not a creative process, and yet it is the process, along with random genetic mutations, that must carry the entire neo-Darwinian theory of biological evolution.[13]

Third, *encoded information, not chance, directs cell chemistry today, and this appears to be a necessary precondition for biogenesis as well.* The present demonstrates what the past can and cannot be. DNA establishes the pattern of biological life, not the other way around. Randomness and chaos in chemistry have no means of producing the encrypted information that would be necessary to direct protein activity at biogenesis. The proper information must be there before the necessary organization to implement this information can be achieved. Without this active information in place and without a system to recognize, read, and implement the information, the chemistry of the cell would remain not only simple but dead.

Fourth, *the necessary source of codes and information retrieval systems is precisely what is not found in nonliving matter.* The four elements of the genetic code, like letters of a genetic alphabet, do not carry messages in isolation. The information is carried only by complex patterns. Even if encrypted information were randomly generated, a sophisticated and complex mechanism that could function as an intelligent receptor system would be necessary to read and decode the information, and this decoder must be in place from the beginning. In fact, the decoder likely would have had to be there first, or else the random encryption could never have been recognized as information, and thus it would have had no standing that could have led natural selection to preserve it. Naturalism has a less effective explanation for the rise of the necessary decoding system.

Fifth, *under no known conditions does information arise spontaneously from noninformation.* This fact is considered by naturalistic philosophy to be in dispute, but the data we have continues to sustain this position, and there is no substantial contrary evidence. Where real information exists, there is an intelligent source. An intelligent perceiver may create meaning where none exists, but in every case information is linked to intelligence.

Therefore, *evolution by mutation and natural selection is not an acceptable theory of biogenesis or of the development of modern life.*[14] The late twentieth-century mind, however, considered naturalistic materialism to be the only worldview that did not set limits on scientific research and the only view that offered a program for research. Natural science, supposedly, can research only those aspects of reality that are within the bounds of the physical matter/energy world; thus, the modern naturalistic scientist often rejects nonnaturalistic worldviews to the extent that they affect his or her research. Theism, or even idealism, will always maintain that some truth and some essential aspects of reality are in principle inaccessible to exclusively empirical scientific research, but theism does not suppose that one is thereby limited inappropriately in terms of research, nor would theists agree that there is no supporting evidence for their view. In fact, they argue that the overwhelming preponderance of evidence and data collected by all honest scientists everywhere fit better into a design model than into an evolutionary model.

The ultimate issue, then, as always, is a philosophical one, but no worldview should be defended with strictly abstract or purely logical reasoning alone. Proving naturalism false is not enough by itself to prove theism true, but the evidence against naturalism is at least partially the evidence that points to theism. The universe, and in particular life itself, is uniquely and effectively understood better by the theistic form of intelligent design theory. A worldview such as theism must effectively interpret scientific data as well as spiritual experiences if it is to be considered as true by the very minds given to men by the God of whom theism speaks.

CHAPTER 7

WHY NOT ADVANCEMENT?

IF MAJORITY OPINION RULES, then the worldview of the advancement rules modern thought life. There are good reasons, however, for advocating a minority opinion. An alternative view is not proven worthy of acceptance merely by showing negative features of the dominant view, but valid criticism does provide some motivation for considering other possibilities.

The assumption that makes criticism possible is directly related to the relationship between truth and reality. The correct worldview is the one that does not contradict, misunderstand, or deny any part of reality. The comprehensiveness of worldviews is complete. Thus, the correctness of one excludes the possible correctness of another. The biblical God cannot both exist and not exist. The natural process cannot both be and not be the ultimate source of reality.

To prove one worldview false is not by itself enough to prove another one true, but it is a valuable preliminary step in such an argument. If a worldview can be shown to be internally contradictory and thus self-defeating, it is thereby shown to be false because the affirmation of a self-contradictory position is in itself a denial of that position. Many may continue to believe such a view, or they may continue to interpret facts from within such an interpretive framework. They will do so, however, because they are unaware of the contradiction in which they are involved or because they deliberately resist the alternatives proposed.

Not much can be done with someone if he understands that his viewpoint is self-contradictory and yet he, nevertheless, affirms it anyway. Such an affirmation would be irrational. Therefore, rational argument would be useless, for reason and the rules of logic would have already been abandoned.

As a practical observation, such irrationality is almost always selective. No one is consistently committed to that which is absurd. *Consistent absurdity* is itself a contradiction of terms. Beyond that, however, for someone to attempt to affirm irrationality consistently would demand that he fully understands what rationality is. How else could he consistently make irrational affirmations? He would have to know what the rational affirmation should be in order to be sure that he denied it properly. Otherwise he might accidentally affirm some rational position. Consistent irrationality is not an actuality in the world of ordinary people.[1] Irrationality is selective; that is, one only affirms irrational positions when one rationally chooses to do so.

Those points at which people choose irrationality usually are not arbitrary, nor are they random. They are, instead, somewhat predictable. For example, people act in their own selfish interest as a rule even if it means acting irrationally, and they resist views that challenge their own assertion of autonomy.

Reason tells us that driving too fast is dangerous, that smoking is unhealthy, that beverage alcohol is harmful in large quantities, yet reason is often ignored if it conflicts with selfish desires. So in other areas, including intellectual beliefs, viewpoints are often rejected because they conflict with selfish desires. These desires are not always bad in themselves. They may include the desire for family or community acceptance. (Many in Jewish or Islamic homes, for example, feel that they cannot even consider the claims of Christ, not only because they think it would be wrong, but because of the threat such beliefs might pose to their security.) Unfortunately, many

Christians also isolate themselves from hostile ideas because they unnecessarily lack strength and confidence in their own faith.

The real problem comes, however, when people see the irrationality of some particular belief they hold, yet they hold it anyway. Defiance of reason is in this case rationally incurable. Therefore, to address the question of alternative worldviews, one must assume the audience to be those who affirm irrationality out of ignorance. In other words, criticism of a worldview is effectively directed only to those people who hold it but do not realize the implications of their own view. One who already sees clearly that the view he or she holds is self-contradictory is not likely to be swayed away from holding that view simply because someone points out that it is a self-contradictory view.

A worldview may be judged at many levels. It may be internally contradictory and thus false. It may also be judged inadequate in the sense of not being able to account for all of the valid data of human experience. Major worldviews, however, are characteristically able to interpret data, though some do so more easily than others. The worldview of the advancement is particularly suitable for interpreting data, and this has attracted many fine minds to it, but it is not without its weaknesses.

The End of Inevitable Progress

A central tenant of advancement thinking, as we have seen, is the idea of inevitable progress. Progress, however, does not characterize every technological or historical advance. The twentieth century saw the greatest advance in scientific knowledge ever known by mankind, together with an unparalleled rise of existential despair. Existentialists themselves often attributed the rise of their viewpoint to the rapid growth of technology and the accompanying depersonalization of modern life.

One cannot ignore the implications of the rise of modern art and hard rock music.[2] Loss of meaning, random abstraction, dissonance, and pagan eroticism are not signs of advancement even upon advancement assumptions. It signifies rather the loss of order, a return to randomness, the destabilization of life, a degeneration from the past. Do advancement theories adequately explain this widespread phenomenon?

"Future shock" theories of psychological depression due to rapid change surely have some merit, and the affect of such change is often similar to the well-known culture shock experienced by those who travel internationally or even from one section of the United States to another. But is this future shock theory a proposal that can adequately account for the direction taken in this century by art, music, and philosophy? Theories of inevitable progress must at least be modified to explain the apparent decline in happiness that so often accompanies the increase of luxuries.

Medicine is a field of rather obvious progress. Today hundreds of diseases have been overcome by new vaccines and antibiotics. Diagnostic procedures are increasingly sophisticated and accurate. Yet costs spiral upwards, hospitals remain crowded, and human life is cheapened. Why do medical advancements not empty the hospitals? Why does the eradication of one disease seem to be followed by massive outbreaks of some other equally devastating plague? We conquer polio and smallpox only to face cancer and AIDS.

With marvelous advances in the treatment of defects and other birth-related problems, why does the deliberate abortion rate rise to unprecedented proportions? If human life is the pinnacle of evolutionary achievement, how can it be so acceptable to so many to terminate a human pregnancy because of the so-called social inconveniences that a baby's birth is thought to cause? That abortion is increasingly acceptable to modern people demonstrates again the prevailing relativism of advancement thinking.

This dramatic shift in attitude so noticeable in the 1970s, 1980s, and 1990s represents a trend that is exactly opposite to cultural advances. It is a sophisticated return to selfishness and to a self-destructive set of values.

It seems to be a general principle that both good and evil accompany technological advance. This can easily be seen with atomic power. The benefits are potentially so great for energy production. Yet the scientific breakthrough in understanding came in work leading to the production of a bomb of enormous destructive power. As scientists learn more about the atom, they learn more about ways to use atomic power for peace, but at the same time, what they learn also enables them to build even more devastating bombs. Even the peaceful use of atomic energy can lead to a Chernobyl. Good and evil arise out of the same technological advance.

Illustrations of this principle can be multiplied easily. A stick can help a blind man walk safely, but that same stick can be used to club an old woman so that she can be robbed. Fire can cook our food, or it can burn down our house. So it is with human inventions. They can be used to help or to harm. Scientific breakthroughs provide basic knowledge that often can be used for peace or for war. Electricity is truly a boon for human civilization, yet it is deadly. Radio can spread the good news of salvation in Christ, or it can spread satanic propaganda. Movies can entertain us, or they can degrade us. It is not at all clear that technological advance is coexistent with progress.

In the natural world time does not obviously produce progress. Things change, but they do not necessarily get better. The fossil record demonstrates that many highly sophisticated and apparently well-adapted creatures have become extinct. Extinction may be due in some cases to rapid environmental changes; nevertheless, it can hardly be seen as a sign of progress. Extinction as a process seems rather to be a loss of order, a clear sign of decline.

In our world today legitimate concern is expressed over the length of the official list of endangered species. Extinction is an irreplaceable loss, not a means of new species production. In the past there were many well-adapted, sophisticated life forms that no longer exist. Nature in the past was more varied, perhaps more beautiful, and seemingly more organized than it is today.

This kind of evidence does not fit advancement theories. Or at least it can be argued that the dominant worldview today is not demanded by all of the facts. Some of the facts point to contrary conclusions. Progress is not inevitable.

The End of Historical Advancement

Modern men, seemingly, have been misled by the rapid increase in technological sophistication in recent years, but the roots of advancement theories are probably historiographical. In other words, first there was a shift in the prevailing theory of history; then the foundation was laid for a shift in cultural interpretation. Instead of history being seen as a straight, level line, it was viewed as a rising curve. Ancient men were assumed to be primitive, whereas modern man was civilized and advanced.

This enlightenment historiography is clearly seen in philosophers such as Kant and Hegel, but archaeological studies have shown that ancient civilizations were actually enlightened and sophisticated. Thus, the idea of ancient people as primitive was simply pushed back further and further until *primitive* became synonymous with *prehistoric*.

While ancient people did not enjoy the technological advantages that we do, they were not primitive in their mental capacity. We must remember that technology builds upon itself, and even a genius in the ancient world could not achieve more than his or her historical context would allow. Ancient people were not primitive in mental capacity. They simply had not yet developed sophisticated energy sources. They had no history of technological development, no effective methods of informational publication, storage, or retrieval, and no distribution system for the preservation of their discoveries. Thus, early developments were slow.

The printing press has often been called the key invention of the modern world, and it is not hard to see why. Reference books are absolutely essential for modern scientific work. Computers, of course, have revolutionized the concept of reference books and mathematical computation. The speed and accuracy available through modern computer technology have made it possible even for average minds to work at levels that surpass the minds of genius quality in the past. All of this stands on the shoulders of the great thinkers of the past, however. Our abilities depend upon theirs.

However, this is advancement only in the sense that the quantity of available, and thus useful, information is increasing. Knowledge advances, but individuals still begin with "two plus two" and the alphabet. Electronic tools enable us to process information rapidly and accurately, but human problems remain the same. Humans may journey to the moon, but they must carry their atmosphere and their food from earth. Moreover, sin remains in the heart of modern people just as it always was in the heart of ancient people.

Advancement is a metaphor that applies to time or to the increase in the quantity of knowledge or to the rise in technological sophistication. Nevertheless, in those essential qualities of humanness, mankind has not advanced. We are still human, with amazingly great abilities and human weaknesses that are equally amazing. Historical advancement is not inevitable or permanent. We can destroy all we have achieved in one great nuclear flash. The self-centeredness of humankind is a self-destructive characteristic. For these and other reasons, many have come to question the doctrine of natural historical development, and thus again the modern worldview fails to describe reality adequately.

The End of the New Beginning

Modern life today is undoubtedly different from the way it was in the past, but in many of the most basic and most essential ways, it is not appropriate to see progress as an inherent feature of all change, and furthermore, it is not by any means necessary to accept the relativism of the modern view which does seem to be inherent within it. Relativism is clearly a result of the loss of truth. When one affirms a view that is logically unable to affirm truth as such, then one is affirming as true a view that by definition cannot be true in any final sense. Such an affirmation is self-contradictory and thus false.

According to the modern view, all evidence for traditional, biblical theism is ambiguous. This is because one cannot know whether God exists if one works strictly within the intellectual framework of advancement thought. Under the earlier view it was easy to know that God existed. Stable kinds demand an origin. Cosmological and theological reasoning led directly to the existence of God; that is, the classical proofs were considered to be rationally adequate. Yet today the same arguments seem to be ambiguous. The modern view cannot accept that older form of thinking. It is skeptical of theistic evidence, and modern scholars delight in showing what they consider to be logical gaps in the traditional reasoning.

It is important to realize, however, that the shift from the earlier view to modern naturalism today did not result from a shift in the nature of the evidence. The shift is in how logic and reasoning are used today to interpret the evidence. Naturalism is not a necessary interpretative model; it is simply a preferred model for some. Teleological (purposive) interpretations of biological or physical data are not inconsistent with the facts. Intelligent design as an interpretive model does not deny any of the facts observed by scientific researchers. Design simply implies the necessary existence of God, a notion currently out of favor, and thus teleology is repudiated, disallowed, or at least avoided.

Arguments that are used in modern attempts to show that cosmological evidence does not lead to the truth about the existence of God are the same arguments that deny the validity of knowledge of the external world in any area—for example, Kant's repudiation of any valid ontological leap from thought to reality. A first cause is implied by the actual existence of contingent beings. If this is not so, then even the most careful reasoning is invalid when applied to reality. If reality cannot be known fully and correctly by rational thought, then science is also condemned to opinion rather than truth. Once again, modern naturalistic science is found to be built upon a skeptical, or at least a relativistic, philosophy. This loss of truth is self-defeating if it is ever affirmed.

Thus, modern people live in a world where they selectively choose what to believe. Some things cannot be believed or even said because they are politically unpopular, not because they are false. Some beliefs are required if one is to be allowed to teach in the modern university. These beliefs are often conformist, nontheistic beliefs, and alternative theistic ideas are disallowed until and unless one first builds a scholarly reputation based on the acceptance of the politically correct worldview assumptions of one's colleagues. In all areas that are not essential to the structure of the modern worldview, scholars are free to choose their beliefs as long as they are careful not to affirm anything that would challenge the basic assumptions of the modern worldview. The advancement rules, and within that framework one is only allowed the freedom to refuse to interpret any facts in any way that might deny the basic elements of the modern worldview.

This attitude is clearly applied to Scripture itself by advancement theologians. Modern theology, though bound by a critical orthodoxy of sorts, is not bound to creedal affirmations. Thus, one can find innumerable patterns of doctrinal belief among professional theologians.

This, however, is not the diversity Paul talks about in 1 Corinthians 12:14–26, for there the different parts make up one body, a true unity. The lack of unity is the aspect of modern thinking that so noticeably sets it apart from traditional, biblical, Christian views. There we had diversity within a common submission to the teachings of the Bible, which themselves were seen in terms of unity. Modern theology has only diversity within the consensus of relative and changing critical opinion.

Today *love* is a key word for the secular world. The music, the books, the speeches of modern men and women are filled with calls for love; but it is an impatient love, a short-suffering love, a feeling rather than, as it is biblically, an unselfish activity directed toward others for their benefit.

Advancement thinking stands in radical contrast to biblical thought patterns. The modern view does not grow necessarily out of the facts available. It is relativistic. It is self-defeating. For these reasons among others, advancement thinking should be abandoned.

CHAPTER 8

WHAT THEN ARE WE TO BELIEVE?

ADVANCEMENT THOUGHT seems to fail at critical points. It is internally inconsistent, empirically inadequate, and lacking in satisfactory explanatory power.[1] The world is in fact designed for life,[2] and life is designed for the world.[3]

Modern minds do not shift easily to an alternate worldview, however. They usually find themselves confronted with enormous peer pressure to maintain naturalistic assumptions. As long as their machines work and their crops grow, it seems like too much trouble to rethink worldview issues. Moreover, the alternate premodern theistic view contains the specter of accountability to a divine being. It does not support autonomous human libertarian freedom,[4] and it strikes at the heart of the spiritually monistic new age.[5]

The Testimony of Ancient Wisdom

Everyone recognizes the enormous benefits that have come from modern science. Better transportation, better kitchen appliances, better medical treatments, better communication systems, better everything! What possible motive could there be to oppose this?

Let's be clear about this. The theistic objection to modern evolutionism is not an objection to technological advance. While some have withdrawn from modern culture, many more—including most evangelical Christians—have embraced modern technology and culture. The objection is not to science itself, nor is it to technological advance. The objection is to advancement philosophy—that is, to the naturalistic worldview—but if this worldview has been the source of the good things of the modern world, why not embrace it?

There are several reasons theists, and evangelical Christians in particular, do not embrace advancement philosophy at this point. First, they do not think that naturalistic philosophy is essential to the technological advance we all applaud. There is a more important reason, however: the significance of human life is at stake.

The great religions have one notion in common. The Judeo-Christian claim is that mankind is made in the image of God—that is, God is the greater, the more, the original; and mankind is the copy, the less, the smaller. It is a unique and wonderful distinctive to be in the image of the great God, but it is also humbling. The life we now have is from a greater life. Our wisdom is made possible by a prior, ancient, infinite wisdom. Our complexity is a lesser reality than the complexity from which we came. Our freedom, our moral responsibility, our intellect, our spiritual life, our significance are granted by and follow from an infinitely good and powerful God who is an adequate source for all human significance.

Islam also understands mankind as being the lesser in comparison to Allah's more. Hindus speak of the individual Atman that somehow reflects the all-pervasive Brahman. A Buddhist seeks a little Buddha in every grain of sand. The greater is reflected in the individuals. The wisdom traditions of the world all speak this way.[6] Human beings are less than their source though like their source in significant ways.

The modern worldview reverses this relationship. Naturalistic evolution says we are the more, and we arose from the less. We are more complex, more significant, more valuable than our source. We arose not by intentional plan but by chance. We are not better than our source by design but by accident. We have an intellect that arose somehow from no mind at all. We have a personality that arose from utter impersonality. We are greater, more significant, more advanced, and our weaknesses come from our ancestry. Our ultimate, original source was not alive; it was simply in process, and even that process was a fluke of instability that unintentionally began a process that unintentionally produced us.

These two pictures cannot be harmonized, no matter how hard one tries. The great world religions find mankind's origin to be from something greater than ourselves, whereas naturalistic philosophy finds our origin in something vastly simpler than ourselves. It simply can't be both ways.

Theistic evolution tries to have it both ways, suggesting that God worked through nature to move along a process from simplicity to complexity and thus created us. This can hardly be seen as anything other than evolution by intelligent design, however, and naturalism would object that this theory only hides the real causes, thus leaving science without the ability to know why anything happens. Christians, on the other hand, believe God revealed that he had uniquely created mankind and placed him over the animals as a creature of a different kind—thus the special creation of the woman from the bone and flesh of the man rather than from another animal or even another mound of dust. Together man and woman stand as a unique kind of creature, together in the image of God, as lesser copies of God's greater being.

Mankind is made from the chemicals (the dust) of the earth (the ground), but mankind is not fully explained by that which is more simple, impersonal, and nonliving. Earthly dust is simple and impersonal and nonliving, but the active source that gave life to the dust could not have been simple, impersonal, or nonliving. Mankind is not evolving up to be gods or to be God. Mankind was brought into being by a God who was already there. Mankind is able by divine intention to rule and have dominion over the earth, and this expectation is not a future hope but was an original status for mankind.

The issues here are fundamental to human self-understanding. Darwinism's contributions to data collection and technological advance can and should be noted with appreciation, but as a world-view it is a step in the wrong direction. It is not the true description of human origins. It is not a valid basis for law, morals, or freedom.

Three Fundamental Truths

Certain basic truths underlie reality. There are at least two of these basic truths, and I would say three. They correspond to what *is* and to the way things *are*. These truths are essential elements of reality itself. They are not merely rational constructs; they are objectively true. They are not only elements of orderly thinking; they are aspects of that which exists. They are not merely statements about reality; they are statements descriptive of reality. The first is:

God exists.[7] Granted his existence is unique in kind; nevertheless it cannot be properly denied.[8] God is the actual and only credible source of all other existing things. His existence is unlike all other existence in that it is not contingent upon its relationships. In other words, God is self-contained and capable of absolute independence. He cannot be described in terms of limits that are appropriate for and applicable to finite reality.

Classical theologians have often spoken of God in terms of what he is *not* rather than in terms of what he *is*. For example, God is said to be infinite in all of his attributes, but this says only that he is not correctly understood as being limited in any aspect of his being in the way finite beings are limited.

Such language leads to interesting mental puzzles, such as whether God could make a rock so heavy that even he could not move it. Either answer, yes or no, seemingly limits God. Or a more sophisticated problem can be stated: Is God's memory limited to those events that have actually happened? Or a more interesting question: Is God's knowledge of the future limited only to those things that will actually happen? We need not be concerned, however, that the limitations implied by such logical problems threaten God's existence, for his existence produces the puzzles.[9]

If God can do anything, can he cease to exist? Answering no does not limit God's existence. Rather, it affirms his eternal uniqueness. To apply strictly finite categories of thought to God and then assume that he *must comply* with what we think the divine nature *must be like* or *must do* is to err from the beginning.

Logical problems with our understanding of the nature of God's existence do not in and of themselves challenge God's actual existence. At best they may point out difficulties with our ideas about God's existence, but in essence they simply remind us that negative attributes are not positive descriptions.

Evidence or sufficient reasons for believing in God's actual existence come not from our ability to solve all problems of logic and language. Guidance for believing in God's existence comes from three major sources. In simple terms, these evidences are: (1) The nature of the universe that exists is wholly contingent and in no sense necessary, in either form or substance. (2) Mind, rationality, and a spiritual nature exist in humans (since mind does not exist in nature itself, nor is mind reducible solely to chemistry or to natural processes), and (3) The unique spiritual experiences that form the historical basis for Christian faith are real, documented, and testable through historical analysis and through personal spiritual conformational experiences. All of these arise from or within the second fundamental affirmation.

The world exists. Using the term *world* here to mean the entire universe, not merely the earth, we discover that the second fundamental truth is different from the first. We plainly see, hear, touch, feel, smell, and taste the world, but we do not always encounter God's being in such ways. At least we do not do so at our initiative. God may (and has) at times chosen to manifest himself in ways our senses can discern, but that revelation is at his discretion, not ours.

We interact with the world in orderly, describable ways. In one sense the same is true of our interaction with God, but we cannot directly study God himself. We can only study his self-revelation.

That is perfectly adequate for knowledge of God, but we do study the world directly, and it is immediately present to our senses.[10]

We seemingly share common experiences with others who also interact with what seems to be the same world.[11] Actually, there is a substantial amount of evidence that this is in fact the case. The world is existing, and we are existing within it. Our existence is contingent upon the existence of our environment. The environment is contingent upon plant life and certain chemical reactions. The seasons depend on an annual orbit of the earth around the sun, and time itself is measured by this and other processes. The accounts of the experiences of a vast majority of others conform to this account, and there is little if any counterevidence.

The existence of this world, however, is not self-explanatory. All parts of the world seem to be contingent upon some other part or parts. None stands alone. Everything is related to something else in such a way that it depends on that relationship. What would the earth be without the sun? What would we be without the earth? And so forth.

Finally the question must be, can the whole be different in kind from its parts? If all of the parts are a contingent kind of reality, is not the whole also contingent? If the answer is yes, then the whole needs a context, an environment, a source of existence. This fact (if it is a fact, and it seems highly likely that this description of reality is true) is then evidence for the necessity of the existence of a God like the biblical God—that is, a Creator God, one whose existence is not contingent upon some part of the universe but who exists in his own right as the Maker of heaven and earth.

The point is that such a chain of dependent existence, as is manifested by the universe, is incapable of existing independently. There must be an ultimate context, and this ultimate context cannot merely be another level of contingent reality. The existence of the "world that actually exists" demands the existence of a "God kind" of being: a necessarily existing, independent being. One is self-deceived to think otherwise.

This ultimate being is thus real but not easily described in the categories of this world. The existence of God is necessary even though he is not seen, smelled, touched, heard, or tasted at our initiative. Two major lines of evidence for God's existence are now evident: He seems to be logically necessary (we cannot rationally conceptualize an infinite series of causes; we rationally conclude that "natural" cause-and-effect chains had an original sovereign cause), but he also seems to be actually necessary. Not only can we not reason our way to God, but the kind of world that actually exists requires an existing causal context with a divine nature.

A third kind of evidence for God is thus capable of being considered, even by the skeptic. Christians claim that this existing God has not merely created and sustained the universe but that he has also revealed himself within it. God has acted within history. He has spoken to individuals and sent them to report his words to others. He has manifested his power in a series of events following and corresponding to those words thus revealed and conveyed.

Where, you say, is this evidence found? Remove your advancement bias for a moment. Forget also all of the irritating and raspy preachers you have heard, and approach the issue not in terms of objectionable personalities but in terms of your own personal quest for truth. Where is this evidence found?

In its sober and stark reality, the answer is in certain old manuscripts from the Middle East. A people contextually enveloped in polytheistic bigotry claimed to have been approached by the Creator of all things. His law was revealed to them through a mysterious intellectual giant named Moses. That law later was completed and fulfilled through Jesus of Nazareth. This righteous individual died on a Roman cross but was seen and verified as having been restored to life in the most unique of all events—his personal, historical, bodily resurrection.

Evidence for this is, historically speaking, more than adequate.[12] His teachings are confirmed in a way unprecedented for any other teacher. The sometime foolishness of his followers through the years is no argument against his uniqueness or his truthfulness.

God exists; the world exists; and *Jesus is Lord!* These are the fundamental truths.

Final Answers

The careful reader at least by now knows the questions. Is the premodern worldview actually more descriptive of reality than the modern advancement view? How could so many of the leading thinkers of the modern era be wrong? Would not a return to a more traditional worldview threaten the status and progress of modern science?[13]

These are good questions, and the answers are straightforward. Yes, in one sense the premodern view is more descriptive of reality than is the modern. To argue that the world is the whole of reality denies both the basis of reality (God) and the focus of history (Jesus). Ethics slide from what ought to be to what is, and the consequences are less than comforting. With no *ought,* we have actions without guidelines. It is like trying to play football without sidelines, yard markers, or referees. The game could not maintain its order for long, nor would it long retain its enjoyable character. We may play by memory for awhile, but the disintegration is inevitable when the going gets rough.

Thermodynamics is a well-established science. It firmly supports the doctrine of naturally rising disorder and thus threatens any doctrine of universal inevitable advance. In fact, it threatens even limited instances of advance unless there is an open system, a protected environment, and an efficient mechanism for energy conversion. Progress and increased complexity are normally and naturally produced by intelligence imposing its will on matter. This is exactly what a theistic creationist suggests as a better explanation for the origin of life than the naturalistic models of biogenesis. Only a person presupposing that nature is all that exists is forced to a naturalistic origin of life.

Some may threaten us with charges that theism is antiscience, but this is simply not the case. Christian faith can only gain from an application of true science to human problems. God's work is no less valuable than God's Word. Scientists or politicians without God's Word to guide them may be deceived into thinking that an unborn child is not a child or that disease is an evolutionary process related to natural selection. Then what happens to medical research, to relief efforts in areas of famine and plague, and to the Hippocratic Oath (to do no harm)?

Rather than fearing that a return to a premodern worldview will threaten the continuing development of science, we should recognize that the modern worldview is self-destructive. The earlier theistic view fostered science and meaningful research for centuries and provided the incentive for purposeful progress. Its moral guidelines naturally enhanced the development of science. The loss of this worldview, more than any other single thing, threatens to dismantle science, to reduce it at best to engineering, and to lead us into a high-tech world without meaning and without norms. We do what we can do. Ethics no longer apply.

Loss of God as an essential part of one's life and worldview is a loss of the only sufficient foundation for meaning, hope, and significance. Without God as a control center, everything floats on a sea of relativity. The hum of the naturalistic subatomic world has no melody; it is either random or uniform, and in either case it is without meaning. Without a key, a decoder, or a foundational purpose, there is only incessant motion and random fluctuations. Is this really a satisfactory explanation of an ordered world arising from the process?

No, it is not. The world exists, but the world is not autonomous. It depends on another kind of reality, one of a different order of reality, one that does not depend upon yet another level of reality but which itself is the ultimate level of reality. This absolute being is properly known as God. Thus the proper worldview affirms both God and the world as existing realities, with God as the more basic of the two.

The place of Jesus is, of course, less clear since there are several rivals. Others claim to be divine spokesmen or enlightened ones, but the claims of Jesus actually exceed them all. His disciple, John, claims that Jesus was God in the flesh.[14]

He could be a liar, though that hardly fits his character or his teachings. A liar who taught only truth! A liar who said, "I am the true and living way"! A liar whose disciples persevered to the death to maintain his claims as being the truth! A liar who warned of judgment based on "every idle word"! No, it is not likely that he could knowingly be a liar.

Was he then self-deceived, a fool, a person who believed his own stories but who learned upon death that he was no different from anyone else? Again, it seems less than credible to argue for his self-deception. All accounts of his dialogues indicate sharp and perceptive wit. He often seemed to know the thoughts of his opponents before they spoke. His mind was clear, alert, and quick with logical argument in debate. He gives no appearance of self-deception.

If he is not self-deceived, and if he is not a liar, then is it not reasonable to assume that he is telling the truth, and that he is God?

Why should it be surprising that God might communicate with us by visiting in and speaking through a human body. God's source-kind of being, seemingly, is not as conducive as it could be to the opening of direct channels of communication, but an incarnation is a perfect solution and an effective means of permitting us to know and hear him, up close and personal.

An incarnation reaffirms the biblical testimony. The life Jesus lived was in fulfillment of Old Testament biblical prophecy. His life was unique in many other ways as well. He affirmed the reality of the world and of God. He addressed each of us with ethical norms that will improve our lives if followed but that will crush us if they are rejected and ignored.

Jesus truly is the focus of the truth about God and the world. He was "God in the world" reconciling the world unto himself.

Some readers will remain skeptical, some will wish to hear more, but some may believe. These are the classic responses (cf. Acts 17). Only the believer, however, knows the truth that sets one free.

CONCLUSION

AUGUST 12, 1981, THE FIRST IBM PC quietly appeared. This was not the first computer, but it was a milestone nonetheless. Computing jumped from the fringes to the mainstream center of popular culture. Like a bridge we crossed so quickly, never to return! Thus was our entrance into the information age. Economic and social transformations over the last two decades have been so great that we can find no parallels in history by which to measure the change. So pervasive did computer technology become, the calendar change from 1999 to 2000 was seen as an enormous threat, something that potentially could have shut down our technological infrastructure due to the simple fact that our most sophisticated computers were counting years using only the last two digits. How would computers know that 00 meant 2000 rather than 1900?

The computer problem was fixed, however, and the millennium bug was avoided, but within a year the financial crash came anyway as the digital fetish faded. Tech stocks for a while pulled the entire world economy into a tailspin. Technological advance continues, however, and the rate of advance seems to be ever increasing.

Seemingly, the inner compulsion personally to possess the latest, greatest, fastest PC has withered somewhat in the male heart, but the escalating power of computers soon will dwarf anything known by even the most sophisticated geeks of the last decade of the twentieth century. Serious futurists are unhesitatingly speaking of a second scientific revolution. Computers broke the ice by mapping the human genome. Computers fuel the fire of biotechnological advance.

Nanotechnology and robotics are advancing at an accelerated pace. Digital technology is changing science, industry, entertainment, and communications. Virtual reality is rapidly becoming an alternate world which will coexist with the old reality.

John Heilemann describes the short-term prospects of the second PC revolution by noting that "the scale of these [anticipated] advances is nearly unfathomable. . . . The dilemmas posed by the second-order revolutions won't be simply economic but ethical, moral, even spiritual; they will cut to the core of what it means to be human. And they will compel us . . . to re-examine some of our most deeply held convictions."[1] He is thinking about the impact of digital technology on the Human Genome Project, cloning, transportation, clean power, and an unexpectedly new, always on, high-speed, everywhere Internet.

Nevertheless, by far the most significant merger of information and life sciences is in genetics and molecular biology. Heilemann quotes Tom Kalil, a Clinton technology advisor: "Genetic engineering might lead to a caste system, with classes of genetic haves and have-nots, or to someone creating designer pathogens to infect millions of people with a deadly disease."[2]

Referencing Peter Schwartz, Heilemann argues that all science is now information science. The microchip has changed everything. The looming and inevitable political conflict, therefore, will be between the secular and the sacred.

Quoting Schwartz, Heilemann muses:

> Cloning, life extension, genetic manipulation, super-intelligence, sentient robots—this stuff has a way of really freaking people out, because it touches on fundamental issues of human identity. What is a human? Are we God-endowed or just chemicals? If I succeed in growing a cell out of chemicals, what does that say about God? If I can manufacture an iris or something even more beautiful, what does *that* say about God?

Schwartz believes the conflict is so fundamental and profound that the time will soon come when "people will kill one another in large numbers as a direct result of the advancement of science."[3]

Hopefully such a bleak outlook will prove to be wrong, but we are all being propelled into a future that seems to be creating itself. The backlash has already begun. Europeans are increasingly concerned about genetically modified foods. Americans are more alarmed by the prospects of human cloning. Technology, of course, is far ahead of the public concerns, and the pace of the advancement is accelerating.[4]

*****

Advancement thought is like bait, attractive to the hungry fish but with a hook in it. It captures the mind but leads to despair. Eventually it undermines the technology that makes it at first appear to be the truth.

Christianity has passion and experience, but it also has superior intellectual content. This content focuses on Jesus, not on the various Christians who for good or ill make up Christian history.

Science gained from biblical faith a demythologized world, a world operated not by unpredictable gods and goddesses but by unchanging, understandable divine laws. Science, to its credit, demonstrates the complexity and the simplicity of the mind of the Creator. God is the personal, purposive source of the underlying order of nature.

History rides on time, and the past is God's reality, as is the future. The Bible warns that support for truth will decline as we near the final judgment, but God's faithful, the elect, will always be able to recognize the essential truth as God has revealed it.

May there be many others who are not ashamed to proclaim allegiance to the name above every name, Jesus of Nazareth, the Christ, our Savior. He alone deserves the title, Sovereign Lord.

ENDNOTES

Introduction

1. The reader should not conclude that the days of the creation week prior to Adam are any less real because of the focus here on history as an account of human life. The events prior to Adam's creation were not events of his experience or of his ancestor's experience, since he had no ancestors, but they were events at least in the lives of angels, and depending upon one's view of time and eternity, they may have been events for God as well. Whatever one thinks of that, history is bound up with this unique creature known as humankind, and history is told and valued by humankind. It is mankind's story as the human race remembers it that we call history. It is nevertheless true, however, that history actually is the human story as God knows it and remembers it, and it began "in the beginning."

2. After the first sin, there is, according to the biblical account, a judgment and a promise of salvation but no written set of laws. No explicit covenant conditions are established until several generations pass. Thus, this pre-covenant era seems to test mankind's conscience as a normative moral guide. See Erich Sauer, *The Dawn of World Redemption* (Carlisle: Paternoster Press, 1964), 63 ff.

3. The human conscience was originally shaped by divine character. A conscience in the image of God would not be a weak norm, nevertheless it failed to restrain wickedness sufficiently. Human rebelliousness and jealousy overcame the testimony of conscience. Though the testimony continued in the form of guilt feelings based upon true moral wrongs, deceptive guilt feelings also appeared due to violations of custom and habit and other less-secure moral norms. The need increased for divine moral guidance and regulation.

4. Memory of this historical event is preserved in the many versions of the Genesis flood account found in the lore of almost all ancient people groups worldwide. An excellent summary of these traditions is found in Byron C. Nelson, *The Deluge Story in Stone* (Grand Rapids: Baker, [1931] 1968), 165–90. See Frederick A. Filby, *The Flood Reconsidered: A Review of the Evidence of Geology, Archaeology, Ancient Literature and the Bible* (London: Pickering and Inglis, 1970). See also the excellent summary and annotated bibliography in Arthur C. Custance, *The Flood: Local or Global,* vol. IX of *The Doorway Papers* (Grand Rapids: Zondervan, 1979), 67–98. Acknowledgment of these traditions is also found in popular sources such as Graham Handcock, *Fingerprints of the Gods* (New York: Crown Publishers, 1995), 187–99, and in serious scientific sources such as William Ryan and Walter Pitman, *Noah's Flood: The New Scientific Discoveries about the Event that Changed History* (New York: Simon & Schuster, 1998), 45–51, 238–52 [though I must add that I think Ryan and Pitman in the end found a truth but misidentified it as the biblical flood].

5. (1) The original pair; (2) Noah and his family; (3) Abraham and his family.

6. A classic study of ancient concepts of time and space is Mircea Eliade, *The Myth of the Eternal Return* (New York: Pantheon Books, 1954). See also David W. Bebbington, *Patterns in History* (Grand Rapids: Baker Book House, 1990) for a review of the nature and impact of a biblical view of time and history.

7. Some evidence of ancient technology is of particular interest to modern researchers, and it is probably false to say that ancients had no advanced technology. Their knowledge, as astounding as it was, however, did not produce a lasting technology. W. C. Dampier, in *A History of Science,* 4th ed. (Cambridge: University Press, 1977), writes: "At an early stage, men almost universally took a wrong path. . . . Some order in empirical knowledge appears in the records of ancient Egypt and Babylon. . . . But the first to submit such knowledge to rational examination, . . . the first to create science, were the Greek nature-philosophers of Ionia" (p. xiii). See also R. Hooykaas, *Religion and the Rise of Modern Science* (Grand Rapids: Eerdmans,

1972), and Christopher Kaiser, *Creation and the History of Science* (London: Marshall Pickering, 1991).

8. An excellent resource for an overview of the people and the issues involved is Jacques Brunschwig and Geoffrey E. R. Lloyd, eds., *Greek Thought: A Guide to Classical Knowledge* (Cambridge: The Belknap Press of Harvard University Press, 2000).

9. This is not to deny that Rome also found occasion to persecute Christians, but one must not think of that persecution as a consistent and universal, much less a perpetual, policy of the state. It was horribly severe when it came, but it was episodic and far less consistent than what Christians in certain parts of the world face today. A good summary of the status of the Christian churches in the Roman period may be found in Bruce L. Shelley, *Church History in Plain Language,* 2nd ed. (Dallas: Word Publishing, 1995), esp. 37–45.

10. Serious students will want to review Norman F. Canter, gen. ed., *The Encyclopedia of the Middle Ages* (New York: Viking, 1999).

11. Though modern scholars seldom refer to it, the most readable history of ideas and cultural development continues to be Will and Ariel Durant, *The Story of Civilization,* 11 vols. (New York: Simon and Schuster, 1935–1975). While a good case can be made for tagging the year 1500 as the beginning of the modern era, and also recognizing 1700 as perhaps another reasonable date for the initiation of what is known as the modern period, the focus on the 1800s and the 1900s is more than simply an American perspective, though the rise of North American culture is undeniably critical to any historical understanding of the contemporary world.

12. Scholars debate the nature and time of this shift. No doubt the Second World War was the most significant event of the modern world, but the 1950s do not show the cultural shifts evident in the famous 60s with its flower children, peace movements, psychedelic drug culture, civil rights struggles, and national crises and triumphs (a president assassinated and a man on the moon).

Nevertheless, it seems that it was the effect of the 60s (not the 60s themselves) that produced the most significant decade of change. Michael Schaffer, in the cover story, "The 70s: Staying Alive," in *U.S. News and World Report,* 2 July 2001, 16, correctly notes that the 70s were years of *progress* and *innovation.* "For better or worse: women entered the workforce in huge numbers, the old family order collapsed, liberal economic orthodoxy got put on the shelf, and the Christian right began to rewrite the script of American politics." Schaffer recalls the subtle impact of Billie Jean King beating Bobby Riggs in a tennis match. The combined effect of Vietnam and Watergate, he says, was massive disillusionment. The tax revolt of 1978, the rise of Bill Gates, credit cards, niche markets, and cable TV: the list goes on, and the case grows stronger that the shift so noticeable by century's end occurred in the "invisible" 70s, the "me generation." From jogging to designer jeans to organic farming and health foods, we remain *I'm OK–You're OK* people: children of the 70s.

13. In general, "postmodern" is a designation of the late twentieth century. The word itself has no meaning other than the trivial one of temporal position, but it has come to be filled with meaning by association. See Craig Van Gelder, "Postmodernism as an Emerging Worldview," *Calvin Theological Journal* 26/2 (1991); and Stanley J. Grenz, "Star Trek and the Next Generation: Postmodernism and the Future of Evangelical Theology," *CRUX* (March 1994): 24–32; David S. Dockery, ed. *The Challenge of Postmodernism* (Wheaton: BridgePoint, Victor Books, 1995); Walter Truett Anderson, *Reality Isn't What It Used to Be* (San Francisco: HarperCollins, 1990); Norman F. Cantor, *The American Century: Varieties of Culture in Modern Times* (New York: HarperCollins, 1997); Millard J. Erickson, *Postmodernizing the Faith: Evangelical Responses to the Challenge of Postmodernism* (Grand Rapids: Baker Book House, 1998); Stanley J. Grenz, *A Primer on Postmodernism* (Grand Rapids: William B. Eerdmans Publishing Company, 1996); Lawrence Cahoone, ed. *From Modernism to Postmodernism* (Downers Grove: InterVarsity Press, 2000); Thomas S. Hibbs, *Shows about Nothing: Nihilism in Popular Culture from the Exorcist to Seinfeld* (Dallas: Spence Publishing, 1999); Edward Gene Veith, *Postmodern Times: A Christian Guide to Contemporary Thought and Culture* (Wheaton: Crossway Books, 1994); Alister E. McGrath, ed. *The Blackwell Encyclopedia of Modern Christian Thought* (Oxford: Blackwell, 1993), s.v. "Postmodernism," by R. Detweiler.

Chapter 1: The Worldview of the Advancement

1. Plato (c.427–c.347 B.C.), one of the greatest of the ancient Greek philosophers, taught that a spiritual world of universal ideas existed. These ideas were the original forms on which all physical reality was modeled and by which physical reality was shaped. Ultimate reality was exclusively rational and thus could be known by the rational human mind even apart from sensory experiences. Medieval Christianity was not strictly Platonic (since Plato taught that the universal ideas were abstract, impersonal, and autonomous), but it was generally Platonic in style. Medieval theologians held that universal ideas existed, but they located them exclusively in the mind of a personal God. Nevertheless, the emphasis was on a separation between spiritual reality above and physical reality here below. This kind of dualism often led to a depreciation of the physical and an exaltation of the rational (the spiritual). Monastic orders illustrate this tendency by withdrawing from the world in order to be more "spiritual." The lifestyle of a stereotypical monk was one of mystical asceticism or otherworld-liness. Medieval art often reflects this dualistic worldview. An introduction to Plato may be found in W. K. C Guthrie, *A History of Greek Philosophy,* Vol. 4 (Cambridge: University Press, 1975), and John Niemeyer Findlay, *Plato and Platonism* (New York: Times Books, 1978).

2. Aristotle (384–322 B.C.), Plato's most famous student, was at one time a tutor for Alexander the Great. Aristotle was heavily influenced by Plato's rationalism, but he ultimately rejected dualism in favor of a materialistic monism that found truth and meaning in particular individual things. Such emphases eventually led to modern, empirical, scientific ways of thinking, but Aristotle's methodology contained many assumptions that depended heavily on common sense or naive observation. These assumptions in some cases prevented scientific progress for many years. For example, Aristotle taught that the natural state of a thing was to be at rest (motionless). His reason for holding this belief was that the earth was the motionless center of the universe (sense perception convinced him of that), and without a causal "mover" nothing would move.

Thomas Aquinas took this "accepted truth" as one of his "five ways" to know that God exists. For many years the apparent motion of the heavens was accepted as a solid proof of God's existence. Who else could move all the stars together with such perfect regularity? This common-sense notion about motion was so obvious that it was not until Galileo and Newton that the modern, more dynamic picture of the universe began to emerge. The modern view has a totally different view of motion. It seems as if the natural state of things is to be in constant motion, and the old "first mover" argument has lost its persuasiveness. For the modern mind there is no longer an absolute, no longer a fixed point; the regular motion of the heavens seemingly is an illusion; the need for a personal mover is no longer obvious. This does not mean that all forms of cosmological reasoning are invalid, but the long-accepted version based on Aristotelian views of motion now seems to have been based on a false premise. For an introduction to Aristotle, see John B. Morrall, *Aristotle* (London: George Allen & Unwin, 1977), and W. D. Ross, *Aristotle* (New York: Barnes & Noble, 1964).

3. Many still do not understand that a free God who is righteous and just is the only reality that can grant responsible moral freedom to living creatures. Only such a being can establish justice and values. Without such a being as the Creator of the universe and of human life, all freedom becomes at best random chance and at worst does not exist. Natural law is inviolable if nature is all that exists. Those who cry for their rights and then advocate a modern naturalistic worldview are simply living in the tension of an inevitable contradiction.

4. See for example, Colin Brown, *Philosophy and the Christian Faith* (Downers Grove: InterVarsity Press, 1968). Key thinkers include Kant, Schleiermacher, Hegel, Kierkegaard, Lessing, Comte, Marx, and Darwin. These men do not necessarily originate every idea that we now associate with their names, but the blend of the teachings of these writers is the intellectual matrix upon which the analytical traditions and the existential patterns of the early twentieth century were built. The postmodern collapse of the twentieth-century castle of naturalism was for many unexpected, but the loss of coherence and normative values in the last decades of the twentieth century reveal the bankruptcy of modernism.

5. It was impossible for Aristotle to imagine how these heavenly bodies could remain in the sky unless they were attached to something.

Since they each had their own patterns of movement, they must each be attached to their own support. Such supporting structures must be round and clear, etc. The system was thus rationally extended, but it depended upon earthbound observational premises.

6. Students have often supposed that the loss of this central position was the great theological crisis that the Roman Church feared if Copernicus were proven correct. In fact, that fear is a later theory imposed on Rome. A moving earth would be moved by God, and a moving earth would not be so close to hell according to Dante's cosmology; so for the medieval mind, a moving earth would have exalted mankind. The objection to a moving earth was the belief that the theory was false, not primarily a fear of theological loss, though some Vatican theologians believed a moving earth would be contrary to certain Scripture passages. The fear of insignificance was real for Pascal, but it did not affect the outcome of Galileo's trial.

7. Christianity in this case is not a reference to a particular denomination or to any world communion as such but rather to the Christian worldview. In this sense, Christianity refers to the belief in an eternal triune God as Creator, Preserver, and Redeemer of the temporal and contingent world, the universe. This God created the world that actually exists and revealed himself within nature and history. Thus, to discover the scientific truth about the world is to discover something about this rational being who created the world by design.

8. Bible verses that speak of the earth's stability or the sun's motion through the heavens are not contradictions of modern cosmological views. They are either straightforward descriptions of appearances as described by an observer on the surface of the earth, or they are figurative descriptions of nature. No one actually thought rivers would clap literal hands (Ps. 98:8) or that trees would literally sing for joy (Ps. 96:12). Nor did biblical people think of the sun as literally hiding in a tent before rising each morning (Ps. 19:4–6). Nor does Ps. 96:10 make a cosmological claim about the planet Earth as might be seen from some hypothetical vantage point out in space. Biblical people did not have that privileged perspective. The planet Earth is seldom if ever in view in Scripture. That which does not move is the geographical status of a physical location that can be identified by observers standing

somewhere on the surface of the ground. The text is affirming the certainty of divine judgment and the comprehensiveness of God's rule.

9. Martin Luther is said to have opposed Copernican heliocentrism because Joshua commanded the sun rather than the earth to stand still. Luther was wrong on this cosmological point, though he read the words of the Bible correctly. What he did not understand was that the Bible never intended to describe the world from a nonterrestrial perspective, whereas Copernicus and later thinkers were in fact attempting to describe the world from a new nonterrestrial perspective, which they seemingly considered to be more objective. In both cases, however, the underlying assumption was the rationality of God and thus of creation. The simplest and most rational explanation that adequately accounts for the evidence is favored. Luther apparently did not recognize the phenomenological language style of the Bible because he was seemingly unaware of all of the evidential issues for which an account must be given.

10. Adam is not created until the sixth day. The Spirit of God is hovering over the surface of the waters from the dark beginning, however, and from some point on this surface the story is told, even before Adam becomes an observer.

11. The most fascinating account of Galileo's life and work is by Dava Sobel, *Galileo's Daughter* (New York: Penguin Putnam, 2000). Clearly the issues at Galileo's trial revolved around biblical interpretation, but it is equally clear that Galileo was a Christian believer who never doubted the truthfulness of the Bible.

12. Newton's God was not Aristotle's impersonal, Unmoved Mover, however. Newton contended that motion was as much a natural state as was rest. This is his doctrine of "inertia." For Newton the system of motion and gravity is as much a manifestation of God's providence as a system of stability would be. Aristotle (and thus Aquinas) saw motion as a direct manifestation of God's activity. Newton saw motion to be as natural as the state of rest. Thus Newton's "God" was more dynamic and was not threatened by changes in nature.

Copernicus could be right and the earth could move, and no negative theological implications would result. In fact, a God who ruled all of this universal motion by simple, rational (mathematical) laws seemed to Newton to be a far grander God than Aristotle's unconscious Unmoved Mover. That this modern Newtonian view ultimately came to be seen as mechanistic (and thus impersonal) was due to philosophical, not factual, changes. See Nancy R. Pearcey and Charles B. Thaxton, *The Soul of Science: Christian Faith and Natural Philosophy* (Wheaton: Crossway Books, 1994), 71–73, 99–95. See also Peter Aughton, *The System of the World: Isaac Newton and the English Scientific Renaissance* (London: Cassell, 2001).

13. The idea of a "chain of being" seems to have come from Augustine's notion that God (through creation) intended to make creatures of every conceivable kind from the simplest to the most complex. Thus, the variety of created things was seen as a series of beings, each one capable of being classified as a link between two other beings. Each creature, then, filled a niche or served as a link in a continuous chain of reality. This image is still preserved in our references to the lack of transitional forms in the fossil record as being "missing links." Augustine's original notion of a "chain of being" was not evolutionary, however. Each variety of created kinds simply unfolded and blossomed into a multitude of creatures of that kind. The many variations of size, coloring, shape, and other characteristics filled out the possibilities within each kind and thus helped to complete the "chain." This concept of creation was seen as an adequate explanation for variation and change among living things while at the same time affirming the basic stability of nature. See Arthur O. Lovejoy, *The Great Chain of Being: A Study in the History of an Idea* (Cambridge: Harvard University Press, 1936, 1964).

14. See Malcolm McDow and Alvin L. Reid, *Firefall: How God Has Shaped History through Revivals* (Nashville: Broadman & Holman, 1997).

15. This *Aufklarung* or "enlightenment" became the self-image European scholars adopted in contrast to what they now called the Dark Ages, the years since the fall of Rome. Kant is suggesting by this term that modern knowledge had finally exceeded that of the ancients. The term *Enlightenment* covered a range of modern ideas in science, literature, philosophy, and politics. See Michael Delon, *The Encyclopedia of the Enlightenment* (London: Fitzroy Dearborn, 2001).

16. While in table 1 the description of mankind in the modern view is optimistic and self-congratulatory, such views are increasingly being recognized as a delusion by those who most fully understand the true implications of the modern naturalistic worldview. Robert L. Smith Sr., of Howard Payne University, in the H. I. Hester Lectures given at the annual meeting of the Association of Southern Baptist Colleges and Schools held at Charleston Southern University, June 1994, as reported in *The Southern Baptist Educator,* September 1994, 3–5, called attention to this shift in thinking:

> A pall has fallen on our society described by theologian Carl F. Henry as "the Blight of Meaninglessness." Harvard paleontologist Stephen Jay Gould in an interview published in *Time* magazine in May of 1990 entitled, "Evolution, Extinction and the Movies" was asked why he had written that humankind was an afterthought, a cosmic accident. His response was that every species is. The interviewer continued, "So the view of evolution as a ladder with humankind at the top rung is incorrect." Answer: "It is nothing more than a representation of our hopes. We have certain hopes and cultural traditions in the West, and we impose them on the actual working of the world." He was then asked what he thought the reason was for our existence. He answered, "There is as much reason for us to be here as there is for anything else. . . . It's just that what happened is one of a billion possible alternatives. . . ." Another question followed, "Does extinction mean failure?" Gould replied, "Extinction is ultimately the fate of all creatures."

Whatever we think of that interview, it gives us a clear insight into the secular worldview.

17. For example, this is the view advocated by Ian G. Barbour, *Religion and Science* (New York: HarperSanFrancisco, 1997).

18. Gordon D. Kauffman, professor of divinity at Harvard Divinity School, in his *Theology for a Nuclear Age* [(Philadelphia: Westminster Press, 1985), 42], suggests that the traditional concept of God is "seriously misleading and dangerous." He insists that we must reconceive God "in terms of the complex of physical, biological and historic-cultural conditions which have made human existence possible, which continue to sustain it, and which may draw it out to a

fallen humanity and humaneness." God, he says (p. 43) is a symbolic word representing "an ultimate tendency . . . working itself out in an evolutionary process." Humans, however, have been polluting the environment. We now have endangered human life on earth, and thus what we do "can have disastrous consequences for the divine life itself" (p. 46).

19. See John Hick, ed., *The Myth of God Incarnate* (Philadelphia: Westminster Press, 1977); and Michael Goulder, ed., *Incarnation and Myth: The Debate Continued* (Grand Rapids: Eerdmans, 1979).

20. Bernard L. Ramm devotes a major section of his *An Evangelical Christology: Ecumenic & Historic* (Nashville: Thomas Nelson, 1985) to a demonstration of this point (see pp. 18ff and 190ff).

Chapter 2: The Rise of Advancement Science

1. Typical of many others, see R. Hooykaas, *Religion and the Rise of Modern Science* (Grand Rapids: Eerdmans, 1972); Eugene M. Klaaren, *Religious Origins of Modern Science* (Grand Rapids: Eerdmans, 1977); and Stanley L. Jaki, *The Road of Science and the Ways to God* (Chicago: University of Chicago Press, 1978). See also Charles E. Hummel, *The Galileo Connection: Resolving Conflicts between Science and the Bible* (Downers Grove: InterVarsity Press, 1986); Colin A. Russell, *Cross-currents: Interactions between Science and Faith* (Grand Rapids: Eerdmans, 1985); D. C. Goodman, ed., *Science and Religious Belief: 1600–1900* (Dorchester: Henry Ling; John Wright & Sons; The Open University, 1973); and David C. Lindberg, *The Beginnings of Western Science* (Chicago: University of Chicago Press, 1992).

2. One of the most readable histories of science is Vincent Cronin's *The View from Planet Earth: Man Looks at the Cosmos* (New York: William Morrow, 1981).

3. Ernst Haeckel, *The History of Creation* (New York: D. Appleton and Co., 1884), 1:8–10. Modern science has not ignored cosmological origins as Haeckel expected, but modern cosmologists have essentially come to a dead end with the so-called "big bang." Hydrogen, or at least the subatomic particles that make up protons and electrons, seems to have no scientific origin. They just suddenly appear and take on a complex structured form. Neither the structures nor the particles

seem to be eternal, and yet the naturalistic bias is so strong that even face-to-face with an absolute beginning, modern astronomers and astrophysicists still sound much like Haeckel when they deny that science has anything to do with God.

4. Reported by Donald Wesley Patten in *The Biblical Flood and the Ice Epoch* (Seattle: Pacific Meridian, 1966), 10–11.

5. Charles Darwin was not the originator of evolutionary thought, nor was he the heroic figure he is often portrayed to be. His place in scientific history is unquestioned, however, even if his ideas eventually fail as a final explanation. See Peter J. Bowler, *Evolution: The History of an Idea* (Berkeley: University of California Press, 1984); see also Robert E. D. Clark, *Darwin: Before and After* (London: Paternoster Press, 1958); and James Moore, *The Darwin Legend* (Grand Rapids: Baker Books, 1994).

6. See John Durant, ed. *Darwinism and Divinity* (Oxford: Blackwell, 1985); David N. Livingston, *Darwin's Forgotten Defenders* (Grand Rapids: Eerdmans, 1987); and James R. Moore, *The Post-Darwinian Controversies* (Cambridge: Cambridge University Press, 1979).

7. Francis Schaeffer, in *How Should We Then Live?* (Old Tappan: Fleming H. Revell, 1976), 148, cites an article to this effect by Murray Eden, entitled "Heresy in the Halls of Biology—Mathematicians Question Darwin," *Scientific Research*, November 1967.

Chapter 3: The Advancement and the Theory of Knowledge

1. By "epistemology" we mean to include the accepted basis for and even the definition of truth as well as the method(s) for gaining knowledge and understanding.

2. If there is no God in the traditional, theistic sense, then there is no transcendent reference point. There is only human perception and the unknown cause of that perception. What I know about the world is therefore limited to what I or my fellow humans perceive or think we perceive. The pure subjectivity of truth leads necessarily to the acknowledgment of the relativity of individual perceptions and requires the willingness to trust subjective accounts of other individually relative accounts of perception. While the objectivity of the natural world is widely accepted as being self-evident, such a claim cannot

be known to be the case if there is no reference point outside of the individual consciousness at which or by which to compare thoughts and reality. Atheistic philosophy always tends toward relativism, and absolutes are lost in every aspect of intellectual life. Without God as the purposeful Creator of the human mind, that perceptive ability which humans have is itself only a fortuitous result of natural processes. As a product exclusively of natural cause-and-effect processes, the human mind cannot be free to make an objective value judgment of any kind.

3. Not all organic molecules are alive, of course, but life is never present apart from organic matter, and thus the naturalistic theory is that life is somehow caused by or arises from specific kinds of natural interactions between these special molecules.

4. A leap to existentialist faith may allow one to function in a reasonably effective manner, but one must deny the objectivity of reason in order to do so. The one who understands this plunges deeper into despair. Writings by perceptive thinkers such as Camus and Sartre illustrate this point. There is no exit if there is no God. The naturalistic room is sealed without a seam. Moreover, there is no love or good will toward men, because all aspects of human personality fall to the same fate as the mind.

5. Most astronomy even today is based on earthbound observations. Recent data from satellites, the Hubble Telescope, and deep space research probes are interpreted by human beings and by computer programs written by earthbound scientists, and at best our data so far gathered still comes from instruments located within the solar system. This does not make the data invalid. Site visits, however, typically bring new perspectives and lead to interpretive revisions of even the most carefully gathered data from afar.

6. Naturalists don't admit this, of course. See, for example, J. E. Barnhart, *Religion and the Challenge of Philosophy* (Totowa, N.J.: Littlefield, Adams, 1975), 166–211. Barnhart is a very consistent naturalist. His moral theory is that pure selfishness will produce an adequate moral norm. The consistent naturalist really has no where else to go.

7. If the theory of evolution were true, for example, the human mind would be the product of that evolution and would function

strictly according to natural law. The mind would not be a free observer, and thus the theory of evolution could not be known to be true. This theory would simply be the way the mind works, not the conclusion of an independent observer.

8. Observe the emphasis of the college textbook by Henry Jackson Flanders Jr., Robert Wilson Crapps, and David Anthony Smith, *People of the Covenant*, 2d ed. (New York: Ronald Press, 1973), 54ff; and Ralph Elliott, *The Message of Genesis* (Nashville: Broadman, 1961). Otto Eissfeldt, *The Old Testament: An Introduction* [(New York: Harper and Row, 1965), 41] says, "Genesis is thus full of tribal and national sagas." Eissfeldt also identifies within Genesis examples of myth, fairy tale, and legend. For a more balanced alternative, see William Sanford LaSor, David Allen Hubbard, and Frederic William Bush, *Old Testament Survey* (Grand Rapids: Eerdmans, 1982), 68ff; see also Roland Kenneth Harrison, *Introduction to the Old Testament* (Grand Rapids: Eerdmans, 1969).

Chapter 4: Modern Theistic Alternatives

1. See Ronald H. Nash, ed. *Process Theology* (Grand Rapids: Baker Book House, 1987) for a critique. See Ian Barbour, *Religion and Science* (New York: HarperSanFrancisco, 1997); and Ian Barbour, *When Science Meets Religion* (San Francisco: Harper, 2000); and Charles Hartshorne, *A Natural Theology of Our Times* (LaSalle: Open Court Publishing Company, 1967) for advocacy.

2. Several introductions to these new scientific theories are available both at the popular and at the technical level. See, for example, Fred Alan Wolf, *Taking the Quantum Leap: The New Physics for Non-Scientists* (San Francisco: Harper and Row, 1981); David Bohm and B. J. Hiley, *The Undivided Universe: An Ontological Interpretation of Quantum Theory* (London: Routledge, 1993); Paul Davies, *God and the New Physics* (Harmondsworth: Penguin, 1990); John Gribbin, *The Search for Superstrings, Symmetry, and the Theory of Everything* (New York: Little, Brown, 1998); Gary Zukav, *The Dancing Wu Li Masters: An Overview of the New Physics* (New York: Morrow, 1979).

3. Quarks and leptons (by one definition, structureless entities with no internal parts) seem to be the fundamental building blocks of all

atomic particles. Some scientists are suggesting that even smaller units (prequarks) may be the truly elementary particles, but whatever sub-atomic particles there may be, they seem to be universal. The structures that produce the variety of matter and life in the universe still seem best explained by intelligent design. P. C. W. Davies, *The Accidental Universe* (Cambridge: Cambridge University Press, 1982) provides an introduction to these recent scientific theories and asks whether structural reality supports an anthropic explanation.

4. Cf. David Ray Griffin, *God, Power, and Evil: A Process Theodicy* (Philadelphia: Westminster Press, 1976). Griffin believes God (the process) is working to overcome evil. It cannot be done in the short term, he claims, but ultimately God will succeed.

5. Such a reality seems to be mathematically possible. Frankly, when I originally wrote this speculation into the text, I was speaking about what seemed at the time to be only a hypothetical possibility. I did not then know of the serious work being done on string theory by John Schwartz, Michael Green, and others. Their conclusions seem to be that a ten-dimensional reality exists (only four of which expanded during the initial moments of the big bang) and that this new metaphysic will ultimately prove to be the basis for a viable "grand unified theory" so desperately sought by modern physicists. For a simplified introduction to this new subprocess model, see Gary Taubes, "Everything's Now Tied to Strings," *Discover* 7 [(November 1986):34–56]. I would not want to suggest that string theory is correct. The evidence, as I understand it, is only that such a model is possible. Empirical data has not yet, to my knowledge, confirmed this model. The point remains, however, that new models are possible, some are already conceivable, and such models could easily require substantial reinterpretations of the process. A positive theistic spin has been put on many of these new developments by Hugh Ross, a popular Christian science writer. See, for example, *The Creator and the Cosmos,* rev. ed. (Colorado Springs: NavPress, 1995), and *Beyond the Cosmos* (Colorado Springs: NavPress, 1996), and *The Fingerprint of God*, 2nd ed. (Orange, Calif.: Promise Publishing, 1991).

6. For example, see Clark Pinnock, *The Openness of God* (Downers Grove: InterVarsity Press, 1994) and *Most Moved Mover: A Theology of God's Openness* (Grand Rapids: Baker Book House,

2001). See also Roger Olson, "Has God Been Held Hostage by Philosophy?" *Christianity Today*, 9 January 1995, 30–34. See also Gregory A. Boyd, *God of the Possible: A Biblical Introduction to the Open View of God* (Grand Rapids: Baker Books, 2000); and Christopher A. Hall and John Sanders, "Does God Know Your Next Move?" [A debate on openness theology] *Christianity Today*, 21 May 2001, 38–45, and 11 June 2001, 50–56.

7. Freedom is not randomness. Freedom is real in beings made in God's image, but it is predictable that the Judge of all the earth will do right. God is absolutely free, but among other things he is not free to cease to exist, to lie, or to defeat himself. Freedom does not imply that knowledge of that freedom is impossible. Human freedom is far more circumscribed than is the freedom of God, and thus it is far more knowable. God does not deny our freedom because he knows our future. That would only be the case if naturalism were true.

Chapter 5: What Is Naturalistic Evolution?

1. See G. A. Kerkut, *The Implications of Evolution* (Oxford: Pergamon Press, 1965), 6, for a similar list. See also A. E. Wilder Smith, *A Basis for a New Biology* (Einigen/Schweiz: TELOS-International, 1976), 15.

2. Biologists often want to make a distinction between the *theory* of evolution and the *fact* of evolution. The theory has to do with *how* evolution occurred. Currently the theory is that *mutations* are the cause of genetic change. *Natural selection* is then the mechanism for preserving useful evolutionary changes. This theory may or may not be true. It is subject to debate, and alternate theories may be considered. The theory is admittedly weak. If the theory is inadequate, however, why not abandon it and accept a creationist view? The scientists answer, "The *theory* may be in doubt, but the *fact* of evolution is indisputable." By this they mean that taxonomic classifications of all creatures can be made. The range of variability is so great that one can find a series of physical similarities between all kinds of animals. DNA and RNA are commonly found in all living forms.

The assumption is that physical and genetic similarity indicates both kinship and descent. This is what is meant by the *fact* of evolution. These similarities and commonalities do exist. We may or may not have the right *theory*, they say, but the *fact* of evolution remains. A secondary argument for the fact of evolution is the fossil sequence, but the interpretation of the fossil record depends on the broader principle of similarity implying descent. This classic error is the blind spot in the modern evolutionary eye. Similarity can more easily result from intelligent design than from blind evolutionary change. The distinction made above, however, is the explanation for why so many evolutionists have been questioning Darwinism in recent publications. They are not thereby questioning the *fact* of evolution. They are questioning the *theory* of evolution. This is also why critiques of the theory often remain ineffective in debates. We can show that the theory won't work, but many remain committed to the fact of evolution, the taxonomic classification system. They believe evolution in that sense is undeniable, and thus they insist that evolution is the only valid basis for conducting scientific inquiry. Theists, however, are in no way defeated by facts that readily support design theory. Taxonomic classification is one of the most useful tools of modern biology, but it can easily be supported as an expected result of divine creation. It is not as obvious that mutation would produce this result.

3. See the competent elaboration of this point and a case for the complexity of even the simplest possible living cell by Michael Behe, *Darwin's Black Box: The Biochemical Challenge to Evolution* (New York: The Free Press, 1996).

4. The most famous of the so-called transitional forms so far found in the fossil record is *Archaeopteryx*, an animal fossil that preserves the form of a crow-size bird complete with feathers. The fossil was first found in a Jurassic setting (i.e., the age of the dinosaurs) in some limestone in Bavaria. If the impression of the feathers had been noticed early on, the original classification of the creature as a reptile may not have been made, but skeletal features may be fairly interpreted as reptilian. We now have at least six fossil specimens of *Archaeopteryx*. It has been supposed that ancestors of *Archaeopteryx* were *theropods* (hind-leg walkers) or *pseudosuchians* (supposed ancestors for all *crocodilians*). According to Tim M. Berra, *Evolution and the Myth of Creationism* (Stanford: Stanford University Press, 1990), 40–41, "*Archaeopteryx* is clearly intermediate between reptiles and birds. It may not itself be the ancestor of modern birds, and it

may not be precisely midway between reptiles and birds, but it demonstrates the transition—clearly it or something like it, descending from reptiles, was the forerunner of birds." But if *Archaeopteryx* is admittedly likely not the ancestor of modern birds, how does it serve as a transitional form, other than by having some structural features such as a toothed jaw and a bony tail and three claws on each wing, which seem more like reptile features than like modern birds? The feathers are fully formed, however; they are not in some transitional phase; and *Archaeopteryx* has a wishbone and a birdlike pelvis.

Berra admits that *Archaeopteryx* has asymmetrical forelimb feathers like those of all flying birds, but he notes some less birdlike structural features as well. He asserts without supporting comment or evidence that feathers evolved from reptilian scales as a better insulation for the body. Only later did these running, jumping creatures discover that these feathers also—unintentionally, but nevertheless by good fortune—permitted true flight. Berra adds: *"Not to perceive its [Archaeopteryx's] transitional nature is to be willfully blind to the obvious."* Berra is too good a scholar to think that his *ad hominem* comments will carry much weight. Perhaps he means only that one should not speak of its fully developed feathers, its pelvis structure, and its large furcula (breast bone), which classify *Archaeopteryx* as a bird, without mentioning the reptilian skeletal characteristics as well. It is more likely, however, that he means that evolution is to him obvious, and this creature is to him compelling evidence of that fact. To others, however, who remain "willfully blind," it seems as if we simply have a fossil of an unusual, ancient, and extinct bird. For some reason—other than "willful blindness," of course—Berra fails to stress that there is no evidence at all that modern birds descended from *Archaeopteryx* (and some compelling fossil evidence against this claim), and there is no evidence that scales became feathers, and there is nothing beyond superficial morphology to suggest that *Archaeopteryx* is transitional or anything other than a fully developed, true-breeding, extinct bird species.

Paleontologists today are more likely to trace modern birds to *Coelurosaur* rootstock. The recent discovery of *Nothronychus* by Doug Wolfe of the Mesa Southwest Museum in Arizona is the latest candidate for that rootstock [see *Science News* 159 (23 June 2001):

389]. Seemingly there were some early Cretaceous feathered *Coelurosaurs* in China [cf. *Science News* 159 (28 April 2001): 262], but the feathers, beaks, and horns all simply appear in the fossil record fully developed. Berra is even more certain of the lavish evidence he thinks he can point to regarding adaptation and change in the case of horses. However, all he really shows is a series of horselike fossils from various parts of the world. Continuing adaptations to a changing environment of a single kind of animal (if in fact even this is what the "horse" fossils show) is not the same as a transition from one kind of animal into another kind, such as *Archaeopteryx* is supposed to show.

Berra claims that there are many other examples of fossils intermediate between major groups, but one might fairly suppose that he chose the strongest and most convincing ones to highlight in his book. If the others are less certain than these, it may be that one could rather easily dispute the existence of any true transitional forms, surely a serious weakness in a Darwinian model. See Duane T. Gish, *Evolution: The Fossils Still Say No!* (El Cajon: Institute for Creation Research, 1996). Berra's worldview allows him to consider his claims to be facts; however, he unfortunately claims that only "willful blindness" would fail to draw his conclusions. The religious nature of this claim should not be overlooked. The factual flaws that so seriously damage Berra's case are laid out simply and clearly in Jonathan Wells, *Icons of Evolution: Science or Myth?* (Washington: Regnery Publishing, 2000). The fossil horse sequence, the peppered moths, *Archaeopteryx,* Darwin's finches, Haeckel's embryos, and more: none of this evidence stands scrutiny, and the real scholars know it. Only textbook writers continue to perpetuate these myths of science.

5. I am not unaware of the research associated with *amphioxus,* the seemingly headless, inch-long, wormlike creatures whose single set of *hox* genes supposedly more closely resemble those of vertebrates than do *hox* genes in, say, *nematodes.* The claim is that *amphioxus* is an archetypical primitive chordate. However, mammals and other vertebrates have four chromosomes of *homeobox* (*hox*) genes, the so-called "blueprint" genes, whereas *amphioxus* has only a single set and only ten DNA fragments as opposed to thirteen *hox* genes in vertebrates. But since certain *hox* genes in each of the four chromosomes

in mammalian cells resemble those in similar positions in the other chromosomes within the same cells, it has been proposed by evolutionists that the multiple sets may have arisen by duplication. Some *hox* genes in *amphioxus,* according to these same theorists, look as if they too may have arisen by duplication of other *hox* genes in the same set.

Thus, the speculation is that gene duplication may be the key to explaining the major steps in evolution, such as the vertebrate/invertebrate division. See *Science News,* 146 (20 August 1994), 116. While I find this evidence interesting, it simply is not real evidence for evolution. Certain possible similarities based on morphological and/or biochemical studies, including studies of the *hox* genes, do not make a transitional form. At best *amphioxus* has some genetic features that may be similar to certain features found in vertebrates, but this is debatable, the similarities are not definitive, and in any case similarities do not by themselves prove ancestry or descent. That is simply an assumption of the evolutionary model for interpreting biological facts. *Amphioxus* remains a true breeding invertebrate creature, not a form in transition. It has never yet been observed producing vertebrate offspring.

6. Intelligent design theorists would not be defeated by such an event, however. The design model could not be defeated by the success of an intelligently designed experiment in a controlled setting. Design theory notes that this context is precisely what the naturalistic model denies about the natural world. If any intelligent scientists prepare and design an experiment in which they cause an organic system to adopt a particular pattern that we consider to be alive, it would not prove that random nonintelligent changes would in time produce the same result. Time is as likely (in fact it is more likely) to produce less order and more disorder. Such is the world of real science.

7. Clearly the assumption of naturalism frames the issues in favor of the naturalistic methodology. This is how worldviews work. Some naturalists believe their naturalism is simply a methodological stance. Others take it to be a fact of reality. In either case it has the appearance of neutrality, but it is not neutral. At root it is a rejection of the possibility and/or the actuality of the existence of a Creator God. This is certainly true in popular culture, but increasingly we see that

naturalism has its own culture and its own agenda and its own variations. See Phillip E. Johnson, *Reason in the Balance* (Downers Grove:
InterVarsity Press, 1998).

8. Proteins have a stereochemistry. The amino acids in proteins are
exclusively *levo* rather than *dextro* amino acids, and yet all experimental evidence shows that any naturally occurring supply would be
racemic (mixed). Thus, the odds against an exclusive selection for a
long protein chain of only one of the options in a natural mixture are
so high as to be virtually impossible. If fact, any combination that is
not exclusively of the so-called left-handed (levo) type will not serve
life at all. The existence of proteins that live provides no support for
theories of protein origin as a result of chance but does provide a
strong reason to accept an intelligent design model. Recent observations of spontaneous groupings on terraced surfaces is interesting but
indecisive. A predominance of levo remains insufficient. Naturally
occurring amino acids are always mixtures, and thus the stereochemistry prevents the spontaneous appearance of life; if it did occur,
it would be far more likely to die or be destroyed by the environment
than to live. Why do advocates of this theory complain that theists
believe in unobservable miracles?

9. See James F. Coppedge, *Evolution: Possible or Impossible?
Molecular Biology and the Laws of Chance in Nontechnical
Language* (Grand Rapids: Zondervan, 1973), 155 ff. The level of
complexity required for even the simplest protolife form is much too
great to be at all likely merely as a result of natural processes. See also
Michael J. Behe, *Darwin's Black Box: The Biochemical Challenge to
Evolution* (New York: The Free Press, 1996) for an explanation of his
concept of irreducible complexity—the idea that life even in its simplest form is already extremely complex; structurally complex in a
way that cannot be explained by chance.

10. This is, of course, only generally true, for in many actual cases
the weak survive. This is easily explained by the design model since a
designer would be likely to build in a strong life force and a will to
live. A naturalistic model does not so easily account for the resistance
to death that characterizes the living world.

11. Christian apologists have strong arguments to make for the
unity of the Creator, but one might not discern that unity simply from

similarities in life forms. The likelihood of multiple designers originating the same genetic code, however, is not high. Convincing arguments against multiple gods were often made by early Christian apologists. See L. Russ Bush, *Classical Readings in Christian Apologetics: 100–1800 A.D.* (Grand Rapids: Zondervan, 1983).

12. It is clear that five and seven are the foundational principles. Genetic relationships and physical similarities could be a result of a creative design, and thus the heart of naturalism must be assumption five. If such a thing happened, however, how could the naturalist know it was not a supernatural act? There is no obvious way to know that what appears to be absolutely spontaneous could not be the result of a supernatural cause.

13. This is not to deny the impact of the dialogue generated in the public arena by the late twentieth-century intelligent design movement, but university textbooks and professional journals have closed ranks, so to speak, and have given no voice to any nonnaturalistic alternatives. See, however, Phillip E. Johnson, *Darwin on Trial*, 2d ed. (Downers Grove: InterVarsity Press, 1993).

14. See Phillip E. Johnson, *Darwinism: Science or Philosophy?* (Richardson: Foundation for Thought and Ethics, 1994).

15. Henry Morris made this point in *The Troubled Waters of Evolution* (San Diego: Creation-Life Publishers, 1974). See Pattle P. T. Punn, *Evolution: Nature & Scripture in Conflict?* (Grand Rapids: Zondervan, 1982), esp. 275–91; but see also Russell Maatman, *The Impact of Evolutionary Theory* (Sioux City: Dort College Press, 1993); and Phillip E. Johnson, *The Wedge of Truth: Splitting the Foundations of Naturalism* (Downers Grove: InterVarsity Press, 2000).

16. We can define *nothing* by listing all possible descriptive attributes and then affirming that those attributes are absent, or we can name all possible forms of substance and exclude them. True nothing, however, has no referent. Using an empty place in outer space as an example of nothingness is an intriguing analogy, but it will not hold because *space* is defined as a specific place through which something may pass to reach another place. It is not "nothing." In fact, outer space is filled with radiation and is defined in terms of distance between objects. None of this is truly nothing.

17. The current theory is that about thirteen billion years ago an instability in the previously stable quantum matrix appeared, resulting in the rapid formation of hydrogen, helium, and perhaps a small amount of lithium, and that this formation process produced a hot expansion (the so-called big bang) which then rapidly inflated according to what appears to be a preexisting template of physical structures and patterns (the physical laws), forming a universe and a collection of stellar objects that produced the heavier elements and initiated a distribution of those elements thus forming the universe we now have. See John Barrow, *The Origin of the Universe* (New York: Basic Books, HarperCollins, 1994). There are alternative theories, such as Eric J. Lerner, *The Big Bang Never Happened* (New York: Times Books, Random House, 1991). Most scientists follow Barrow over Lerner, but the consensus is not unanimous. A simplified review of several viable current proposals was published by *The New York Times* on the Web, 22 May 2001. See "Before the Big Bang, There Was . . . What?" by Dennis Overbye (http://www.nytimes.com/2001/05/22/science/22BANG.html).

18. In fact, as reviewed in the previous footnote, modern science believes these processes were at one point initiated spontaneously without outside intervention, and the processes produced an enormous universe that is still in process and still growing.

19. It is important to realize how dependent naturalistic theories are on the notion of self-causality. Every causal chain leads back to some beginning. The origin of all processes is either some other natural cause, which simply begs the question, or a spontaneous event that is either a self-cause or an uncaused cause. A self-caused event is conceivable—magnetic attraction, for example—but self-caused existence is not. Something cannot cause itself to exist if it is not yet existing. Something that does not exist is nothing, and nothing is not a cause of anything. An uncaused cause, however, is conceivable, though it could not be a natural reality experiencing universal change and process. Intelligent design theory does not face this problem, because it is not committed exclusively to natural causes.

20. Energy alone is not self-organizing, however. Something must capture the raw energy from the sun and/or from other sources, and direct, convert, and/or organize that energy to serve as food, strength,

consciousness, or whatever. The complexity of such energy-capturing and energy-organizing converters is the secret flaw in modern biology. A cell capable of capturing and using energy is a complex reality, and yet this energy-conversion system must already be in place if we are to have the spontaneous rise of complex cells. Chlorophyll, for example, must precede viable green plant life, and yet that is exactly what it cannot do.

Chapter 6: Why Not Naturalistic Evolution?

1. Not all things are actually discovered by following the so-called scientific method. A whole range of things now confirmed as true were originally discovered more or less by accident. See Royston M. Roberts, *Serendipity: Accidental Discoveries in Science* (New York: John Wiley and Sons, 1989). Why this would be so remains something of a mystery if naturalism is true.

2. James Rachels in *Created from Animals: The Moral Implications of Darwinism* (Oxford: Oxford University Press, 1991) persuasively argues that if humans are not biologically special, then neither can we be morally special. It is difficult to find a flaw in this reasoning. Therefore if Rachels is wrong, it must be because his premise is wrong.

3. It must be noted, however, that even noncreationists have begun to express an increasing dissatisfaction with traditional evolutionary theories though not necessarily with the naturalistic worldview. For example, see Michael Denton, *Evolution: A Theory in Crisis* (London: Burnett Books, 1985); and Michael Pitman, *Adam and Evolution* (London: Rider, 1984). Fred Hoyle and N. C. Wickramasinghe in *Evolution from Space* (London: J. M. Dent, 1981) suggest that it is more reasonable to believe that the earth was seeded from space than to believe life evolved on earth from nonliving matter. Hoyle's book sets forth a compelling case, as does Denton's, for the impossibility of standard evolutionary theory serving as a satisfactory explanation for the facts known to science. These writers do not all advocate intelligent design, but that remains as a reasonable alternative theory. Nevertheless, those with a worldview commitment to a naturalistic theory of origins will fail to find this alternative persuasive (cf. Rom. 1:19–20).

4. Though animals can and do communicate, and some highly advanced animals can learn to use and perhaps understand language signs of another species (e.g., dogs learn to respond to human verbal and physical commands), animals do not naturally communicate in a grammatical language, are not rational or religious, and do not naturally practice interspecies communication except under the training and supervision of humans and then only in limited ways.

5. See Evan Shute, *Flaws in the Theory of Evolution* (Grand Rapids: Baker, 1961); A. E. Wilder Smith, *Man's Origin, Man's Destiny* (Wheaton: Harlod Shaw, 1968); Wayne Frair and Percival Davis, *A Case for Creation*, 3rd ed. (Chicago: Moody, 1983); Lane P. Lester and Raymond G. Bohlin, *The Natural Limits to Biological Change* (Grand Rapids: Zondervan/Probe, 1984); Scott M. Hulse, *The Collapse of Evolution* (Grand Rapids: Baker, 1983); Duane T. Gish, *Evolution: The Challenge of the Fossil Record* (El Cajon: Creation-Life Publishers, 1985); Henry M. Morris and John D. Morris, *The Modern Creation Trilogy* (Green Forrest, Ark.: Master Books, 1996); Henry M. Morris, *That Their Words May Be Used Against Them: Quotes from Evolutionists Useful for Creationists* (San Diego: Institute for Creation Research, 1997); and Allen L. Gillen, Frank J. Sherwin, and Allan C. Knowles, *The Human Body: An Intelligent Design* (St. Joseph: Creation Research Society Books, 1999).

6. Consider the compelling nature of the case presented to the U.S. Supreme Court in 1987 as reported in W. R. Bird, *The Origin of Species Revisited*, 2 vols. (New York: Philosophical Library, 1989). See also Tom McIver, *Anti-Evolution: A Reader's Guide to Writings Before and After Darwin* (Baltimore: Johns Hopkins University Press, 1992).

7. Several authors have published evidentialist defenses of Darwinism, however; e.g. Michael Ruse, *Darwinism Defended* (Reading: Addison-Wesley, 1982); Richard Dawkins, *The Blind Watchmaker* (New York: W. W. Norton, 1986); and Robert T. Pennock, *Tower of Babel: The Evidence against the New Creationism* (Cambridge: MIT Press, 1999).

8. Thus, we are now seeing evangelicals present a few philosophical texts on the subject; e.g., Norman Geisler and J. Kerby Anderson,

Origin Science (Grand Rapids: Baker, 1987); and J. P. Moreland, *Christianity and the Nature of Science* (Grand Rapids: Baker, 1989).

9. This case is made in far more detail and with more expertise by A. E. Wilder Smith, *A Basis for a New Biology* (Einigen/Schweiz: TELOS-International, 1976), 16–32 and throughout the 291-page volume.

10. If materialism or any other form of naturalism were true, then it would be necessary to account for the origin of life from nonlife, personality from the nonpersonal and rationality from the non-rational. Therefore rationality itself is questionable, because it is grounded upon nothing. Evolutionists do believe that life arose from a nonliving reality, but rational beliefs, such as that one, assume that rationality is valid and capable of being true. This basic assumption, however, is exactly what naturalism cannot justify. This inability to support the reliability of reason itself does not mean that it is impossible for naturalism to be the case, but it is certainly an argument against the truthfulness of naturalism. Rationality is essential to any effort to discern the truth or falsity of any claim. Any view that cannot justify rationality is a view that cannot be known to be true. It can be argued that a view that cannot explain why rational thought is better than non-rational thought is a view that is likely to be false.

11. When an animal or a person dies, all of the chemistry remains, and the organization of that chemistry remains, though it begins to deteriorate after death. Maintaining chemical complexity is not the same as preserving life. Simply to arrange chemicals in organized patterns is not to create life.

12. Recent (1999) laboratory experiments with fruit flies have produced two varieties that seemingly do not interbreed. One popular definition of *species* is "an interbreeding gene pool." Thus, some think that a new species of fruit fly has been created through artificial selection procedures. See Richard Morris, *The Evolutionists: The Struggle for Darwin's Soul* (New York: W. H. Freeman and Co., 2001), 212–14 ff. Under such definitions, one may or may not have reason to believe that a new species has been formed by artificial selection, but no one has turned a fruit fly into something other than a fruit fly. Stickleback fish over time seemingly by natural selection became two nonbreeding kinds of stickleback fish in three British

Columbia lakes. The fact that they don't breed is the proof the evolutionist wants, but the fish all remain varieties of sticklebacks. It continues to be correct that no one has produced a new kind of life-form even when they with great effort do succeed in generating nonbreeding types of fish, flies or whatever.

13. Committed Darwinists may protest that artificial selection works with short time spans while natural selection works over long time spans. Time is no ally to random processes, however. A series of chance events is more likely to simplify a system than to complexify it, and even if complexity were achieved, encoded information would not arise spontaneously. Pure chance is as likely to go backward as it is to go forward, and pure chance alone over enough time should result in no status change at all. Supposedly, natural selection preserves the upward flow of useful changes. This is perhaps possible but by no means certain, and to suggest that natural processes successfully preserved the vast number of needed changes while eliminating all others is a confidence that significantly exceeds the evidence. The illusion that time is a friend of complexity has deceived many; it is a greater deception to expect time plus chance alone to produce any encoded information, much less the vast quantity of sophisticated information carried on even the simplest DNA strand. DNA changes that are significant enough to cause a positive change that would be recognized and preserved by natural selection are not likely to be small, point changes. They are rather pattern changes, exactly what mutations almost certainly would not cause.

14. This is not a new argument. The significance of the genetic code in this regard was clearly articulated by A. E. Wilder Smith, *The Creation of Life: A Cybernetic Approach to Evolution* (Wheaton: Harold Shaw, 1970). Points three and four of this critique are capable of scientific study, and points two and five may suggest programs of research. This is a negative rather than a positive argument, and thus it may not be enough in and of itself to cause a change in the dominant mind-set, but it nevertheless points to a serious flaw in the current theory of the origin and development of life offered by naturalistic science.

Chapter 7: Why Not Advancement?

1. I am not denying that brain damage and mental handicaps exist that might lead people to act irrationally. The point being argued in the text is intended for ordinary, average, everyday society: but even in the "abnormal" cases, something can be said. Many types of mental illness or brain damage can be diagnosed correctly because of a regular, consistent pattern of symptoms. The consistency is internal to the malady, and thus within given parameters even the mental antics of schizophrenia or multiple personalities may be said to have their own rationality. We can often learn to "understand" them even though they do not "make sense" to us. Again, however, I repeat, the argument being made in the text is directed not at the exceptional cases but at the ordinary cases, including, of course, those "exceptions among the ordinary" who might have chosen to read this book.

2. Cf. H. R. Rookmaaker, *Modern Art and the Death of a Culture* (Downers Grove: InterVarsity Press, 1970); and Kenneth A. Myers, *All God's Children and Blue Suede Shoes* (Wheaton: Crossway Books, 1989).

Chapter 8: What Then Are We to Believe?

1. Advancement thought assumes that *reason* is a late appearance in the natural process, but then it wants to trust *reason* to explain the process out of which it came. Advancement thought has no data establishing that the world we have actually came about by random mutation and natural selection. At best the argument suggests that the world *might* have come about that way. And advancement thought faces an explanatory impass when it comes to the true nature of the genetic code and its role in the development of life.

2. This point is made in an exceptionally persuasive way by John D. Barrow and Frank J. Tippler, *The Anthropic Cosmological Principle* (New York: Oxford University Press, 1986). See also J. P. Moreland, ed. *The Creation Hypothesis: Scientific Evidence for an Intelligent Designer* (Downers Grove: InterVarsity Press, 1994), and Hugh Ross, *The Creator and the Cosmos* (Colorado Springs: NavPress, 1993), 118–21.

3. See Michael J. Denton, *Nature's Destiny: How the Laws of Biology Reveal Purpose in the Universe* (New York: The Free Press, 1998).

4. In an age of political correctness, one of the best-kept secrets of the modern naturalistic worldview is its total lack of support for human freedom other than by appeal to some fundamental randomness or to a supposed quantum indeterminancy. Only theism posits a fully free Creator who can and does introduce freedom and, thus, moral responsibility into the created order.

5. See John P. Newport, *The New Age Movement and the Biblical Worldview: Conflict and Dialog* (Grand Rapids: William B. Eerdmans Publishing Company, 1998).

6. See Houston Smith, *Why Religion Matters* (New York: HarperSanFrancisco, 2001). This book may well be the most significant critique of naturalism to appear in the first year of the twenty-first century. Smith is a widely recognized scholar who sees clearly that naturalistic scientism is the established religion of the modern academic world, the media, and the law; he believes this is not good for the future of humankind.

7. An excellent summary of the evidence for this claim is found in Terry L. Miethe and Gary R. Habermas, *Why Believe? God Exists!* (Joplin: College Press, 1993).

8. Tillich argues for a concept of God as the "ground of being" rather than God as "a being" (cf. Paul Tillich, *Systematic Theology*, 3 vols. (Chicago: University of Chicago Press, 1951, 1957, 1964). Thus God could not be said to exist since that is what beings do. See also his *The Shaking of the Foundations* (London: SCM Press, 1949). But Tillich does not adequately take into account God's self-revelation. It makes no sense to say that a revealed God does not exist as a being if God acts and speaks and has a name. Nor is it at all obvious how a mere philosophical Ultimate Concern can account for an existing universe. Even recognizing the uniqueness of God's uncreated existence, we still do better to speak of his existence than to follow Tillich's misleading restatement of Plotinian pantheism. See Colin Brown, *Philosophy and the Christian Faith* (Downers Grove: InterVarsity Press, 1968), 191–200, and John Warwick Montgomery,

Where Is History Going? (Grand Rapids: Zondervan Publishing House, 1969), 118–40.

9. It is neither honoring to God nor accurate to propose that God can defeat himself. Denying that God can make something he cannot control is in fact to honor his unlimited ability. It is only human confusion to think of this as a contradiction in the idea of God. God cannot make a rock so big that he could not move it, for to do so would mean that he could defeat himself, which is nonsensical. It would be like saying God could paint himself into a corner and thus be trapped. Or it would be like suggesting that God could blow himself up or divide himself into an infinite number of infinite beings and thus fill infinite universes with each of his pieces. Such conceptions of God do not affirm his real power. God's unity and ever-living nature rule out some logically conceivable scenarios. Far from being a weakness, the unity and strength of God is partly found in that he cannot defeat himself or destroy himself in these ways. The nature of God's knowledge of the past and the future can be stated in interesting (and confusing) ways as well, but the answers given either way do not affect God's existence. Our answers will reveal what we think about God's thoughts, but we can be wrong and God will still be right. He knows what he knows. If he knows every "what if," then we must conclude that alternate realities are knowable. If he knows only the actual past or future, it is no limitation on God unless alternate realities are knowable and God doesn't know them. We have no evidence that this is true, however. Some point to our ability to read novels and fiction. This may lead us to suppose that God would know the plots of all fictional novels, but whether God knows the plots of novels never written or conceived is another matter. Why would he be weakened if the answer is no? The truth is, he might know those kinds of things, and he may know what you would have done if you had acted differently from how you did act, but God's existence and authority and power do not seem to depend on one's answer to these kinds of questions unless one were to argue logically that God does not know actual reality. It would seem to many that God's knowledge of actual reality is plenty to know, but Jesus seemed to know some "what ifs" (cf. Matt. 11:21 and Luke 16:31). Thus, we simply do not succeed when we affirm real limitations upon the divine nature. God knows

whatever he needs to know and whatever he wants to know. Our lack of understanding of how this could be is no limitation on God.

10. Del Ratzsch, in *Philosophy of Science: The Natural Sciences in Christian Perspective* (Downers Grove: InterVarsity Press, 1986), 125–26, notes that Christianity supports, but does not force upon us, some form of realism. God created our senses and our rational mind in such a way that they are appropriate for learning truths about nature. He says:

> Without such a connection between our abilities and truth, some sort of anti-realism would be difficult to escape. A purely naturalistic evolution, for instance, would not provide us with such a connection. Evolution does not necessarily select for "truth of conceptualizations." Survival and fitness depend on having the appropriate characteristics and engaging in appropriate behavior regardless of what one might think one is doing. Darwin himself recognized that, and during at least one stage he worried that evolution might undercut justification for believing in the mind's reliability. Thus it may be that something other than a pure naturalism is needed to justify the realism which predominates in contemporary philosophy of science and which has predominated historically among scientists. God's having created us for this world and having created us as knowing beings certainly gives us a start on such a justification. Such a justification would provide for the possibility of our getting to theoretical truths. Our fallenness might partially explain why we have no guarantees of reaching such truths.

See also Paul Davies, *The Mind of God: The Scientific Basis for a Rational World* (New York: Touchstone, Simon & Schuster, 1992).

11. Could it be that others are in their own world and that we are deceived about the unity of the world because of the seeming unity of the various reports? While such a view could perhaps be proposed for analytical scrutiny, it does not seem plausible, and we reasonably assume that only one world exists and that we share it with others.

12. See Colin Chapman, *Christianity on Trial* (Wheaton: Tyndale, 1975); Norman Anderson, *A Lawyer among the Theologians* (London: Hodder and Stoughton, 1973); Gary R. Habermas, *The Verdict of History: Conclusive Evidence for the Life of Jesus*

(Nashville: Thomas Nelson, 1988); Gary R. Habermas and Antony Flew, *Did Jesus Rise from the Dead? The Resurrection Debate* (San Francisco: Harper and Row, 1987); and William Lane Craig, *Apologetics: An Introduction* (Chicago: Moody Press, 1984), 167–206.

13. Many say yes, but a good case can be made for the compatibility of the ancient Bible and modern field-based science. Four different approaches are represented by the following: Howard J. Van Til, Robert E. Snow, John H. Stek, and Davis A. Young, *Portraits of Creation: Biblical and Scientific Perspectives on the World's Formation* (Grand Rapids: William B. Eerdmans, 1990); Lloyd R. Bailey, *Genesis, Creation, and Creationism* (New York: Paulist Press, 1993); Hugh Ross, *The Genesis Question: Scientific Advances and the Accuracy of Genesis* (Colorado Springs: NavPress, 1998); and Henry M. Morris, *The Biblical Basis for Modern Science* (Grand Rapids: Baker Book House, 1984).

14. John 1:14. See "flesh" in Colin Brown, ed., *The New International Dictionary of New Testament Theology*, vol. 1 (Grand Rapids: Zondervan, 1975). For a summary of the claims of Christ, see Norman L. Geisler, *Christian Apologetics* (Grand Rapids: Baker Book House, 1976), 329–39.

Conclusion

1. John Heilemann, "Second Coming," *PC Magazine*, 4 September 2001, 140.

2. Ibid., 146.

3. Ibid.

4. August 26, 2001, CNN Headline News reported IBM's announcement of their success in creating the first single molecule computer circuit. Nanotechnology with all its promise is here. Will this fire cook our food, or will it burn our house down? If history is our guide, the answer is yes and yes.

INDEX